The Subplot
What China Is Reading and Why It Matters

COLUMBIA GLOBAL REPORTS
NEW YORK

The Subplot
What China
Is Reading and
Why It Matters

Megan Walsh

People's Republic
of China

Published with support from the Andrew W. Mellon Foundation

Published by Columbia Global Reports
91 Claremont Avenue, Suite 515
New York, NY 10027
globalreports.columbia.edu
facebook.com/columbiaglobalreports
@columbiaGR

Library of Congress Cataloging-in-Publication Data
Names: Walsh, Megan, author.
Title: The subplot : what China is reading and why it matters / Megan Walsh.
Description: New York, NY : Columbia Global Reports, [2022] | Includes
    bibliographical references. |
Identifiers: LCCN 2021040999 (print) | LCCN 2021041000 (ebook) |
    ISBN 9781735913667 (paperback) | ISBN 9781735913674 (ebook)
Subjects: LCSH: Chinese fiction—21st century—History and criticism. | Books
    and reading—China—History—21st century. | Literature and society—China—
    History—21st century. | LCGFT: Literary criticism Classification: LCC PL2443
    .W228 2022 (print) | LCC PL2443 (ebook) | DDC 895.13/609—dc23
LC record available at https://lccn.loc.gov/2021040999
LC ebook record available at https://lccn.loc.gov/2021041000

Book design by Strick&Williams
Map design by Jeffrey L. Ward

Printed in the United States of America

CONTENTS

Introduction

"The sky and ocean are crystal clear today,
 much too clear for poetry composition."
 —Liu Cixin, "The Poetry Cloud"

In 2014, Chinese President Xi Jinping informed a room full of
authors, artists, and filmmakers, without a hint of irony, that
"fine art works should be like sunshine from blue sky and breeze
in spring that will inspire minds, warm hearts, cultivate taste,
and clean up undesirable work styles." Echoing Mao Zedong's
famous 1942 *Talks at the Yan'an Forum on Literature and Art*, in
which artists were instructed to serve the people and the Party,
Xi clarified that "modern art and literature needs to take patriotism as its muse, guiding the people to establish and adhere to
correct views of history, the nation, the country, and culture."

This unabashed request for art to project sunshine is no
different from the Chinese Communist Party's impressive, if
cavalier, efforts to artificially control the weather itself; from

the media and government agencies characterizing "smog" as
"fog" to deploying anti-aircraft guns to fire chemical missiles
into clouds during the 2008 Beijing Olympics. Blue skies could
be the literal and figurative emblem of the government's drive to
"tell China's story well." And authors are expected to act much
like a cloud-bursting machine, banishing shadows rather than
seeking them out.

China's authoritarian political climate, on the other hand,
also known as "the weather" or "the gray zone," is intentionally hazy. It shifts in severity according to the CCP's needs,
often without warning, creating a disorientating psychological
landscape for Chinese writers, captured in a short work by the
avant-garde poet, essayist, and novelist Han Dong:

> It's foggy, or smoky
> Perhaps it's smog
> No one's surprised by that (. . .)
> Even on a clear day I can't see roadside trees and
>   flowers clearly
> Even if I see them I don't remember them
> Even if I remember them I can't write about them

This well-documented climate of censorship and propaganda can make foreign readers rather snobby about Chinese literature, often without having read any of it. It's rare for
English speakers to have heard of, let alone read, beyond such
giants of Chinese literature as Lu Xun, Mo Yan, or Liu Cixin.
And while it's not uncommon for translated fiction to struggle
on English-language reading lists, it is impossible to ignore the

fact that the whiff of censorship all too often reduces the arts in mainland China to an academic curio or a worthy totem of fearless political protest.

As a result, Mo Yan's 2012 Nobel Prize in literature was always going to be mired in some kind of controversy. The Chinese government celebrated his—and China's—international accolade, while critics in the West denounced Mo Yan's loyalty to the CCP. Salman Rushdie branded Mo Yan a "patsy of the regime" and Herta Müller dismissed his prize as a "catastrophe." But the response also highlighted the ways in which Western readers, much like Xi's blue-sky imperatives, can also have intrusive and unrealistic political expectations for Chinese authors, especially those for whom "banned in China" is too often the baseline for what is and isn't worth reading. The assumption can be that those who don't openly challenge China's authoritarian system from within are apparatchiks, not artists.

But the fact is that most Chinese writers who continue to live and work in mainland China write neither what their government nor foreign readers want or expect. And in our failure to engage with and enjoy Chinese fiction as it is, in all its forms, we misunderstand our own part in the complex and often fascinating realpolitik at its heart: this intrusive relationship between grand and personal narratives. There is much to learn from Chinese writers who understand and illuminate the complex relationship between art and politics—one that is increasingly shaping Western artistic discourse.

In the last hundred years, Chinese fiction has been asked to do a lot of heavy lifting. At the turn of the twentieth century, reformist Liang Qichao famously declared that renovating

Chinese fiction would "renovate the people." His call was
answered by the exhilarating, anti-Imperialist May Fourth
Movement of the 1920s, which promoted vernacular Chinese
and literary realism as iconoclastic ways to modernize China
and the nation's consciousness. From this point on, literature
and the arts increasingly played the part of agitator, in particular to stir up resistance to the Japanese invasion, the KMT-led
Nationalist government, and colonial influence in treaty port
cities. Then, under Mao, of course, literature became a beast of
burden for socialist propaganda, generating new genres written,
for the first time, by workers and peasants. Mass book banning and burning during the Cultural Revolution halted China's
genuine, homegrown literary production for years. Contra-
band foreign novels by writers like Alexandre Dumas, Gabriel
García Márquez, Charles Dickens, Jorge Luis Borges, and Wil-
liam Faulkner became part of an organic, underground literary
canon. Unsurprisingly, by the time of the Cultural Revolution,
only one writer was sufficiently sunny: Mao himself.* Writers in
the early years of Reform and Opening Up, a series of economic
initiatives instigated in 1978 by Mao's eventual successor Deng
Xiaoping, flooded the void with new genres and experimental
fiction. But this literary Wild West was brought to heel with the
1989 crackdown and massacre at Tiananmen Square.

Understandably, this century of literary boom and bust has
left noticeable scars on China's publishing landscape. Unable
to develop continuously and organically, much of China's

---

* Mao was often compared to and depicted as the Sun. As a result, it was
dangerous to talk of "the Sun going down." As Yu Hua notes, "at nightfall,
the most one could say was, 'It's getting dark.'" Yu Hua (trans. Allan. H Barr),
China in Ten Words (Duckworth Overlook, 2012), p. 22.

14 homegrown fiction is reactive by nature; it carries the ghostly watermark of its time. As a result, the importance and fragility of homegrown fiction should not be taken for granted. Modern Chinese fiction is a mixture of staggering invention, bravery, and humanity, as well as soul-crushing submission and pragmatism—a confusing and intricate tapestry that offers a beguiling impression of Chinese society itself.

In the last decade, since Mo Yan's Nobel Prize, literature has been given a vague new responsibility—to serve Xi Jinping's much vaunted, largely economic project of national rejuvenation, "The China Dream." This dream is forecast to come true imminently, when China's per capita GDP reaches $10,000, the benchmark for a "moderately prosperous" (*xiaokang*) society. *Xiaokang* is itself a literary term, literally meaning "small comfort," and dates back 2,000 years to the *Book of Songs* and the *Book of Rites*, classics of Chinese poetry. It is seen as the prelude in Confucianism to *datong* or "great harmony"—proof, perhaps, that while the leadership attempts to steer writers toward its desired policy goals, literature can have a lasting influence on the nation's political direction without even trying. And a reminder that economic growth requires shared cultural touchstones to translate individual prosperity into a national narrative.

Nevertheless, while China's spectacular era of economic, technological, and scientific advancement has seen the emergence of a booming mainstream, consumer-driven film, TV, and online industry, the publishing world hasn't been able to keep up. Give a quick glance at the last three years of China's bestseller charts, and you'd be forgiven for thinking that little had been written in the last three decades. The majority of

titles are Chinese classics (on school curricula), old novels res-   15
urrected by TV adaptations, and the odd, unexpected foreign
import: Keigo Higashino's Japanese magical realism mysteries
and little-known Scottish writer Claire McFall's young adult
novels both have permanent top-20 rankings.

But this official picture is misleading, largely due to the
reluctance or inability of publishers and booksellers to take
risks on much of what is being written. Like all cultural sec-
tors, they are regulated by the state. The General Administration of Press and Publications (GAPP)—which is controlled by
the Publicity Department of the Communist Party of China*
(CCPPD)—ultimately decides what is permitted, by granting
or withdrawing publishing licenses, while not offering a set
of transparent and specific rules. Works that embrace "core
socialist values" are deemed "harmonious" and "healthy," but
the exact criteria for what that means are not explicit or official.
Instead, the GAPP encourages a culture of intuitive, and sometimes superficial, compliance.

The most prominent entrance displays in even the most
indie-looking bookshops—architecturally sleek urban café-
booksellers are the unofficial symbol of trendy metropolitan
living—are devoted to books about communist history and
its leaders. But that's not to say controversial or critical books
are unavailable. Pass by those obligatory CCP book promo-
tions near the door, and novels about, say, authoritarian governments, by George Orwell or Aldous Huxley, can be found
tucked away inside—even if works by dissident writers such as
Liu Xiaobo and Ma Jian cannot. Foreign novels generally aren't

* In Chinese, the word for propaganda and publicity is the same: *xuanchuan*
宣传.

16 seen to represent or reflect Chinese culture, and therefore are not deemed a threat to it. What is published by Chinese writers in Chinese is of paramount concern.

Which means that some controversial works, if translated into another language, are still available. The translated English version of Chen Xiwo's "I Love My Mum," a story about a sadomasochistic relationship between a mother and her disabled son that has been widely interpreted as a metaphor for deep-rooted corruption in Chinese society, is easy enough to buy. No approved publisher, of which there are about 580, would dream of distributing it in Chinese. Caution within the industry tends to smother anything that could be considered overtly "yellow" (pornographic) or "black" (politically sensitive). Those books require safe ports either in Hong Kong or Taiwan, or with Western publishers.

Most of the time, checks and balances kick in a little earlier. Until recently, membership in the Chinese Writers' Association (CWA), established seventy years ago to uphold "literary norms," has been the main path for writers seeking publication. It is the official gatekeeper of what is known as "pure literature" (usually defined as non-mainstream social realist literary works) even though in practice it is commonly seen as a rather creaky "old-boy network" that operates by "looking at the writer, not the writing." The CWA pays a stipend to members of a certain level, backs editors of magazines such as *People's Literature* and the affiliated website China Writer, and is often assumed to operate a culture of supportive reviews and publication opportunities, not to mention access to prestigious national accolades such as the Mao Dun Literature Prize and the Lu Xun Literary Prize. The current president, author Tie Ning, withdrew her

work from consideration for the Mao Dun Prize after eight of the
ten nominees for the 2011 award were found to be either the chair
or the vice chair of the CWA's provincial branches.

It is important to emphasize, however, that membership in
the CWA is not an act of state collusion but one of convenience.
Many talented and/or controversial writers hold prominent
positions, including Su Tong, Ge Fei, Mo Yan, Jia Pingwa, and
Liu Cixin. It's a crucial reminder that the line between dissident
and collaborator is a blurry one in China. Artist and outspoken
China critic Ai Weiwei was able to design the Bird's Nest sta-
dium in Beijing for the 2008 Olympics, albeit as a local advisor
to the Swiss architectural firm Herzog & de Meuron. The ban on
Zhang Yimou's 1994 film *To Live* was lifted only when he was
asked to direct the opening and closing ceremonies. In reality
the relationship between criticism and complicity is as cloudy
as the editorial demands of the state.

Most controversial writers who remain in China have continued to work, at least up until now. They may not always have
official backing, but unofficially they can do what they want.
"In writing we have freedom, but in publishing we have discipline" said author Yan Lianke, whose editors, not himself, were
punished for printing one of his novels. Chinese censorship has
been described as an "anaconda in the chandelier." The policing
of content is intentionally unpredictable and unnerving, placing
the onus on publishers and writers to second-guess what might
cause the snake to strike from above.

This official unpredictability has given rise to Chinese fiction that is both tenacious and unusual. It has generated inno-
vative literature that Yu Hua believes is written in "the spirit
of May 35," in reference to the way many people in China avoid

18   triggering the censors by referring to the Tiananmen Square
      massacre's date not as June 4 but May 35; it is the literary equiv-
      alent of the knight's move in chess. Many authors have managed
      to hone their style and subject matter in spite of the unpredict-
      able weather. Whether in political rain or shine, the best have
      created unmistakable worlds that are unique to themselves as
      individual writers and endemic to their homeland, as did Kafka,
      Borges, or Faulkner. Despite the challenging conditions, litera-
      ture is flourishing.

          In recent years many young writers, embracing online plat-
      forms or self-publishing fiction, have unintentionally disem-
      powered the literary publishing establishment. Gatekeepers such
      as the CWA, once sniffy about the internet, are scrambling to
      keep up now that Chinese online fiction is the largest publishing
      platform in the world. It is also one of the most insecure—a
      large quantity of Chinese fiction sometimes disappears at a
      moment's notice. A sense of flux pervades many genres, both
      in terms of the restive political weather and the longevity of the
      work itself. It lends a precious quality to the ideas explored, and
      in the last twenty years has given rise to a whole new taxonomy
      of Chinese literature: a vast migrant-worker poetry movement;
      class-conscious youngsters; a stressful generational divide;
      "rotten girl" homoerotics; underground comics; "face-slapping"
      web novels; CCP-friendly corruption capers; and ethnic out-
      sider stories—not to mention what is widely hailed interna-
      tionally as a golden age of Chinese science fiction.

          In 2015, Liu Cixin's science fiction epic, *The Three-Body
      Problem*, became the first novel written by a mainland Chinese
      author to climb both domestic and foreign bestseller charts. It's
      not surprising that science fiction has been the genre to take

Chinese fiction into uncharted territory—the future is itself unmapped and unconstrained by tiresome geopolitical fault lines; it is harder for domestic censors to police and easier for foreign cynics to navigate. In its depiction of alien civilizations mercilessly competing for supremacy in the universe, Liu Cixin's trilogy has been interpreted in liberatingly contradictory ways: as a critique of communism, as a swan song for democracy, or as a parable for the dog-eat-dog world of e-commerce. It is testimony to Liu's skill as a writer that whatever his own views may be, they are not overt and, like most Chinese writers, he will not comment publicly on any political intentions.

At the heart of the novel is the "three-body problem" itself, a famous mathematical conundrum, depicted as three suns whose unpredictable movements flip an alien planet without warning between eras that are Stable (temperate weather in which civilizations grow) and Chaotic (ferocious fire and ice storms during which people hibernate). Despite its fantastical storyline and dense conceptual physics, *The Three-Body Problem*, like much of the best science fiction, is both prescient and pertinent, keeping what Liu Cixin himself calls a kite line to reality.

Out of a seemingly clear sky, the 2020 coronavirus pandemic flipped our own planet into chaos. Governments squabbled in their battle to stabilize both the virus and control its narrative, while hospitals and parliaments descended into havoc. The CCP's political "weather" is always at its most inhospitable during times of national celebration and/or social upheaval, and it's no surprise that in 2021, which marked the hundredth anniversary of the founding of the CCP as well as the ongoing economic and political fallout of COVID-19, that the climate for artists and writers seemed to be entering another ice age.

20   In China, in the grip of drastic lockdown policies and a well-oiled propaganda machine, the early days of the outbreak became a salient reminder of fiction's unique value: nonfiction and front-footed poetry drew too much attention to itself. Projects such as "Terminus2049" (named after a planet in Isaac Asimov's *Foundation* series), which archived online reports of the coronavirus outbreak before they could be deleted, were shut down. "Citizen journalists" were arrested. Flash poetry, the primary source of non–state approved information in the early days of the COVID-19 outbreak, was taken down as quickly as it went up. Often deeply personal and disarmingly simple, these ephemeral poems momentarily challenged the official government narrative, and exposed how it was constructed. "The slogans are yours/The praise is yours," wrote a nurse from Gansu province who volunteered to work on the front line in Wuhan. "The propaganda, the model workers, all yours (. . .)/I just want to return home safe when the epidemic ends."

The government's political exhumation of the arrested whistleblower Dr. Li Wenliang—which included a rare public apology after his death—was skewered by Wang Youwei in an aphorism for state hypocrisy:

> They said during their lifetime
> Please shut up
> After death they said
> Please rest in peace

The most revered and now controversial writer to emerge amid the lockdown was the "battlefield diarist," previously known as Wuhan author Fang Fang, whose daily updates kept alive stories of individual suffering among governmental narratives of triumph. Already an established novelist known for her "Wuhan flavor" and for elevating the hardships of ordinary workers, she has been branded a traitor for her nonfiction, and she received death threats for agreeing to publish the deleted diary abroad.

The domestic backlash to Fang Fang's diary was proof of the brewing nationalism attached to the COVID-19 story itself, bolstered by a petty international blame game and the West's stark incompetence in dealing with the spread. But it also highlighted the power of what was known as the "main melody" to coordinate the nation's mood, as well as the increased awareness of—and the need for—alternative viewpoints when that master narrative presented its fiction as fact.

For many writers, the best way to present inconvenient truths is to do the opposite, to willfully present fact as fiction. When novelist Yan Lianke started visiting so-called "AIDS villages" in his home province of Henan, he had intended to write a field study of China's AIDS epidemic caused by unsanitary and exploitative blood sales back in the '90s known as the "plasma economy." But fearing censorship, he changed tack and wrote a novel instead. The result was *Dream of Ding Village*, a remarkable exploration of a mysterious "spreading fever" that was as much about the unscrupulous role people played in the disease's spread, as it was about the psychological fallout of a hushed-up epidemic. The 2005 novel was banned anyway, but this has not stopped Yan from writing and teaching at a university in Beijing.

Chinese fiction writers are well adapted to extreme shifts in climate, and they deftly navigate an official, state-sanctioned

22   script that undermines the messy truth of individual experi-
      ences. And through their fictional worlds, they remind us that
      these difficulties are far from unique to China. The impact of
      post-truth politics is as global and disturbing as the pandemic.
      When asked in 2019 about China's "re-education" camps in Xin-
      jiang, US Secretary of State Mike Pompeo justifiably defaulted
      to the world's most famous work of dystopian fiction to criticize
      the actions of the Chinese government. "The pages of George
      Orwell's *1984* are coming to life there," he declared. But he con-
      veniently ignored the fact that American readers had sent the
      same book shooting back up the charts after Donald Trump's
      inauguration speech. We turn specifically to fiction for explana-
      tion, solace, and guidance when things feel out of step, or when
      our realities no longer measure up to the stories we are being
      told. It's an existential state that Chinese fiction writers have,
      for decades, learned to sublimate, parody, escape, and confront.
          In 2021, to conveniently coincide with the centenary of
      the founding of the CCP, the China Dream's economic tar-
      gets were forecast to come true. Just as the finest literature
      about the American Dream—the belief in meritocratic suc-
      cess, self-reliance, and that things will always get better—
      almost always exposed its illusory or nightmarish reality, so
      Chinese fiction of the early twenty-first century reveals the
      myriad ways in which writers are telling a different story from
      the one expected or demanded of them. And just as America's
      "Gilded Age" laid the foundations for the century of fiction
      that followed, with the sharp evisceration of rich elites by Edith
      Wharton, the elevation of the working man by Upton Sinclair,
      and the pulpy, dime novels offering tales of dogged survival,
      fluffy urban adventure, or romance, so contemporary Chinese

fiction will provide the cultural foundations for how the rest of
the world understands China in the decades to come.

Works by writers from Taiwan, Hong Kong, and other Sin-
ophone territories are not included in this book, for the simple
reason that their authors in the last century have not been subject to the same political and historical experiences as those on
the mainland. Chinese diaspora writers who now live permanently outside China are also mostly not included—and where
they are, only briefly, on the assumption that they write within
different parameters. The focus is fiction written in the last
ten to twenty years, by writers who live and work in mainland
China. Most, but not all, of the texts mentioned are available in
some form of English translation. It goes without saying that
only a fraction of works published on the mainland are included.
This is not a comprehensive overview, but a glimpse.

Most importantly, this book celebrates the ways in which
literature almost always explores the shadows, often without
trying, nurturing ideas and individuals that wither and die in
the full glare of the Sun. These subplots draw our attention to
unseen impulses that drive the main story, asking us to notice
what has been left out of the spotlight. Only by seeing what is
displaced can we understand the reason that certain ideas and
experiences are foregrounded. In today's confusing and chaotic
landscape, when metanarratives are drowning out individual
voices, and screens large and small compete for our attention,
the diminished status but persistent value of literature has the
ability to both reveal the truth and highlight what is still hidden.

Lost Causes
Out with the Old, In with the New

"Everyone believed in dreams, but didn't believe in reality.
It was all very odd."
—Yan Lianke, *The Day the Sun Died*

Many Chinese writers who grew up during China's largely agrarian, socialist revolution do not feel at home in today's capitalistic, urban society. Not because they long for its return, but because their past seems to have been forgotten, or erased. Unsurprisingly, perhaps, their recent fiction portrays people caught up in absurd states of limbo, often told by narrators who are neither dead nor alive. In Yu Hua's 2013 novel, *The Seventh Day,* a dead man wanders around his city like a stranger, joining hordes of other unburied souls who are also searching for their lost memories and sense of place. And as the man's past begins to emerge, so too does his grief, which he realizes was "nipped in the bud, long before it had had time to grow its natural dimensions." It's an eerie, suspended state echoed by other writers of his generation—Yan Lianke, Mo Yan, Su Tong, Ge Fei, Can

Xue—who all find unique ways to depict people who are trapped in the often farcically unnatural dimensions of a present without its past.

Sometimes referred to as the "lost" or "perplexed" generation, many Chinese writers born in the fifties struggled during China's Reform and Opening Up period to come to terms with what they saw, and what they did, during the Cultural Revolution. As a result, the 1980s became a period of frantic literary innovation—as therapy, exposure, sublimation, and critique—giving rise to genres that included "scar literature," "misty poetry," the philosophical "root-seeking" movement, and the dystopian avant-garde. And yet, following the 1989 Tiananmen Square massacre, this dynamic and cathartic "high culture fever" was also nipped in the bud before it had time to fully bloom.

The political crackdown of 1989 meant that many Chinese writers who were already living abroad, decided not to return, with some of them becoming the leading lights of a politicized diaspora, not entirely dissimilar to America's "lost" writers—Ernest Hemingway, Gertrude Stein, F. Scott Fitzgerald, T. S. Eliot, and later, James Baldwin—"finding" themselves in Paris or London. "A monk from afar knows how to chant," so the Chinese saying goes; distance offers clarity. It also offered the freedom to tackle head-on the political hot-button issues that authors who stayed in China either could not, or would not, touch—at least, not directly.

One of these dissident, exiled writers is Ma Jian, whose fiction almost always zooms into no-fly zones: Tibet in *Stick Out Your Tongue*, the Tiananmen massacre in *Beijing Coma*, and the mass sterilizations and forced abortions of the one child policy in *The Dark Road*. His latest novel, *China Dream*, hits President Xi

26   right on the nose. It concerns a corrupt official trying to enforce
        a dystopian national brainwashing policy in which a microchip is
        inserted into people's brains to replace personal memories with a
        fictional version of Xi's communal "China Dream." Ma Jian's work
        is fearless and inventive, but it also carries the wounds of exile.
        The naked political agenda in his fiction is a poignant reminder
        that, having had to live abroad for more than twenty years, he is
        ceaselessly compelled to critique the authoritarian politics that
        have cruelly prevented him from staying in China and writing
        about it firsthand.

        Compare his novel *China Dream* and Yan Lianke's *The Day
        the Sun Died*, neither of which were allowed to be published on
        the Chinese mainland. Both appeared in English translation in
        2018, when they were confidently marketed as critiques of the
        "China Dream." But unlike Ma Jian, Yan Lianke, who lives and
        teaches in Beijing, denied such claims: "A direct connection to
        'the China Dream' was not what I intended at all. It would actu-
        ally have been rather dangerous for me to go around writing a
        critique of it—and far too simplistic."

        The Day the Sun Died is not a critique of the "China Dream"
        but the strange, lived experience of a waking nightmare. Yan
        depicts a village that has plunged into a dark dream-walking epi-
        demic, in which cause has no direct bearing on effect—no one
        knows where or why the sleepwalking epidemic has emerged. It
        is as if the world and its inhabitants have been body-snatched.
        At the margins, a fictional author called "Yan Lianke" wanders
        around, terrified of falling into the sleepwalking state himself.

        It is true that writers who have stayed in China are unable
        and unwilling to be literal or overt with their politics. But to
        nakedly do so in their fiction would also not be true to their

experience of living there. What was mistaken in the West for 27
Yan Lianke's veiled criticism of "the China Dream" is in fact
a genuine depiction of what he sees and feels around him: an
obscured world that no longer makes sense, politically or
socially, in which people are unaware of their own absurd pre-
dicament, and in which his own identity is fictional, where the
idea of the author is itself part of the fiction.

Writers who continue to live and work on the mainland face
two obvious challenges. The first is the official story, known
in China as the "main melody." All the subjects to which we in
the West naturally and rather doggedly gravitate when writing
about China—the Cultural Revolution and the pitiless violence
of the Red Guards; mass starvation during the Great Famine;
the backyard furnaces of the Great Leap Forward; anti-Rightist
gulags and the suicides and persecutions during Land Reform;
tanks let loose on students—are not up for public or direct discussion. And that's not even including Tibet, Taiwan, Xinjiang,
and, more recently, Hong Kong.

The second obstacle is that, these days, the past really does
feel like another country. China is completely unrecognizable.
The PRC has been literally and metaphorically rebuilt in the
last forty years and in this newly globalized, industrialized, and
urbanized PRC, economic growth has become the new national
narrative. More than 300 million migrants have left rural homes
and flocked to gleaming, newly minted towns and cities. It's
estimated that 800 million Chinese people have climbed out of
poverty. By 2025 China is forecast to become the world's leading
luxury market.

The writers in this chapter, all born in the fifties and sixties,
provide the missing links between two seemingly unrelated

28   eras; their fiction depicts a uniquely honed and endemic vision of what it's like to live in China when a connection between their past and present has been severed. It interrogates what happens to society—and storytelling—when, as Yan Lianke says, "the occurrence of B is completely *unrelated* to A." Not only must these writers live with subjective memories that have no place in official narrative history, but the absence of cause and effect throws their narratives and protagonists into groundless and surreal physical and psychological states.

The most well-known, and perhaps criticized, writer of this generation is Mo Yan, born in 1955 to a peasant farming family in the Gaomi county of Shandong province. His 2006 black comedy, *Life and Death Are Wearing Me Out*, is narrated by a man trapped in a humiliating cycle of reincarnation. The Buddhist king of hell, Yama, presides over a condemned landlord's cycle of rebirth after he was murdered at point-blank range by a fellow villager during the brutal mob violence of land reform. Over a period of fifty years, the man lives and dies repeatedly, reborn as a donkey, then a dog, an ox, a pig, and a monkey. Through their eyes he witnesses twentieth-century China's seemingly relentless political revolutions from feudalism to socialism to capitalism. He is a comically lucid but largely impotent witness.

The role of powerless witness is one that Mo Yan himself knows well; it's how he coped with the controversy surrounding his Nobel Prize in literature in 2012. He spoke of the pain he felt when accused of being a mere mouthpiece for the CCP and expressed a plaintive hope that readers let his fiction speak for him:

Over time, I've come to realize that the real target was
a person who had nothing to do with me. Like someone
watching a play in a theatre, I observed the performances
around me. I saw the winner of the prize both garlanded
with flowers and besieged by stone-throwers and mud-
slingers.... For a writer, the best way to speak is by writing.
You will find everything I need to say in my works.

Mo Yan draws a clear line between his writing and himself
as a writer. And, just like Yan Lianke, he regularly includes a fictional and unsympathetic version of himself within his novels.
In *Life and Death Are Wearing Me Out,* "Mo Yan" is a side character and intermittent commentator. This fictional Mo Yan is
no more than a "braggart" who will "deceive people with heresy,
[who] is in the habit of mixing fact and fantasy in his stories."
The real Mo Yan cautions "you mustn't fall into the trap of
believing everything he writes."

This intentional confusion between writer and writing is
evident in Mo Yan's pen name, which means "don't speak." Mo
Yan has upstanding communist credentials: He is vice chair of
the state-aligned CWA. Along with several other writers, he
publicly copied by hand parts of Mao Zedong's 1949 *Talks at the
Yan'an Forum on Literature and Art,* a set of rules demanding that
all art serve socialism. And he's a veteran of the People's Liberation Army. On the surface, his accreditation makes him just
another cog in the propaganda machine. In fact, he embodies
the political value of silence, having traded his public persona to
some degree for greater freedom as a writer.

Readers of Mo Yan's fiction know that, unlike the soft-
spoken author, his writing is garrulous, feverish, and sometimes

smutty. He rarely paints a rosy picture of rural Chinese life, the setting for all his novels. And his use of magical realism is not whimsical or redemptive, but corporeal and bathetic. His creations include a brutal cattle merchant who can urinate a distance of fifteen meters, a girl whose giant wings make her easier to shoot dead, and starving children who can eat iron.

Pious Western critics should note how often he satirizes or pities people who fanatically support any political ideology. Violence carried out on behalf of the state, rather than out of personal anger or despair, is Mo Yan's own way of depicting the horrors of severed cause and effect. This is no more poignant than in *Frog*, in which a midwife becomes a zealous enforcer of the one-child policy by carrying out thousands of late-term abortions over many years, in some ways just to prove her loyalty to the Party over the nationalist traitor she loved. And Mo Yan relishes portraying peasants and officials at their most mercenary and ridiculous when fervently toeing the party line, such as in *Life and Death*, in which the village builds a Cultural Revolution theme park where people pay to reenact the very same frenzied and terrifying denunciations that had been so hard to witness earlier in the novel. The feckless expediency and baffling amnesia of those trying to get ahead at all times, be it under socialism or capitalism, mirrors the closed cycle of the narrator's monstrous, unending reincarnation in which the effect becomes the cause.

Ultimately, inflexible and performative political zeal is often helpful for Mo Yan's characters, even if the path of sanity seems to belong to those who quietly plough their own furrow. The impoverished, independent farmer who refuses to hand over his small parcel of land during collectivization could sum up Mo Yan's own paradoxical role as frenemy of the state: "I have nothing against the Communist Party and I definitely have nothing against Chairman Mao. I'm not opposed to the People's Commune or to collectivization. I just want to be left alone to work for myself."

If Mo Yan's positioning ultimately enables a degree of self-certainty, Yan Lianke suffers from a sense of self-erosion. One of China's less biddable homegrown writers, Yan Lianke is also one of its finest. Having cut his teeth as a propaganda writer for the People's Liberation Army, he went on to write scripts for the Army's TV production unit until, following his controversial 2004 novel *Lenin's Kisses*, he was asked to leave the PLA after twenty-five years of service. He has since devoted himself to writing (mostly banned) fiction and teaching creative writing at universities in Beijing and Hong Kong. In stark contrast to Mo Yan's deceptive humor and irreverence, Yan's strange fictional worlds are rooted in a radiant and rational sadness.

Yan Lianke describes his work as "mythorealism," literature that depicts "unrealistic reality, a non-existent existence." He believes that only by seeing the absurdity of that existence can one grasp "the wild roots growing under the soil of reality." In other words, his fiction is an imaginative, and somewhat optimistic, attempt to offer up the absurdity of reality in the hope that its causes will become clear. This quest is perhaps most powerful in his 2011 novel *The Four Books*, which questions the role and value of reality itself. The title is a vague reference to the Bible's four gospels and the classics of Confucianism, also known as "The Four Books" (widely seen as the philosophical foundation of classical and modern Chinese

32   thought) and to China's "Four Great Classical Novels" (*Journey to the West, Outlaws of the Marsh, Romance of the Three Kingdoms,* and *Dream of the Red Chamber*). Yan Lianke said he wrote the novel "recklessly" and "without any concern for getting published." The story, set during the time of the Great Leap Forward and the Great Famine, comprises jumbled-up excerpts of four different manuscripts that depict the same horrific events in an anti-Rightist re-education camp, through conflicting perspectives and literary styles. In effect, the subjective, *Rashomon* format mirrors the absurd, splintered, and manipulated narrative of the camp and, perhaps, society itself.

The first "book," a neo-Biblical parody entitled "Heaven's Child"—the name for China's emperors through the ages—is the omniscient, master narrative, and is used here as an allegory for the state. It regales with chilling detachment and poetic license the actions of the camp's needy, sadistic leader, The Child. Two more "books" are written by The Author, a prisoner who exists in an impotent, schizophrenic state, one in which he informs on his fellow inmates to secure early release (a pitifully pragmatic tome called "Criminal Records"), while the other is his private diary of the camp's real horrors, including his own complicity in them (known as "Old Course"). Life in the camp is revealed, fragment by fragment, to resemble a terrifying farce. It is a place in which the rules are arbitrary, including the reasons for imprisonment itself. The inmates' crimes are their professions: The Musician is re-educated for listening to Liszt, The Mathematician for proving that one plus one is *really* equal to two. Their internment has no logical explanation, their labor no effect on their release, which depends on meeting scientifically impossible farming and smelting quotas.

Albert Camus argued in his essay, "The Myth of Sisyphus," that the eternal punishment of rolling a rock to the top of a hill, only for it to roll back down again, was the condition of Modern Man, and that to recognize the absurdity of one's existence was its own salvation. In the closing chapter of *The Four Books*, Yan updates this theory with an excerpt from the fourth "book." An essay written by The Scholar called "A New Myth of Sisyphus" depicts the pleasure Sisyphus finds in concealing from a vengeful god the small pleasures that make his punishment tolerable. He pretends not to love his daily view of a small community in the valley as he heads down the mountain each day. It is not a lesson to love one's servitude, but to disguise and sublimate one's intellectual freedom, to hide it in plain sight. This, Yan seems to be saying, is the condition of modern Chinese artists and scholars.

Mo Yan and Yan Lianke are two very different writers who have lived consciously within metanarratives for much of their lives. Both began their writing careers as "red pens" in the People's Liberation Army, learning ways in which to construct the official story. And they did so in the language they grew up with, *Maospeak,* the idiom-heavy vernacular of state media that some critics argue poisons all art at its source. Invisible in translation, unmistakable in Chinese, *Maospeak* infected the linguistic style and substance of entire generations who internalized overt political doctrine—which is externalized in their fiction through parody. Yan knowingly misuses Maoist slogans, such as *Serve the People!* (the title of his novel about a couple's counter-revolutionary sexual fetishes) and *The Day the Sun Died* (a play on the metaphor of Mao as the Sun). Both authors exploit their early experiences as propaganda writers in their

34   own fiction—namely, that there is never a reliable narrator, not
      even themselves.

The ability to move into the present has been easier for a slightly
younger cohort of writers—Yu Hua, Ge Fei, and Su Tong—who
witnessed, but did not participate directly in, the Cultural Revolution. Unlike Mo Yan and Yan Lianke, over the years these
authors have moved from collective narratives in rural communities to individual experiences in a fragmented city.

Emotional detachment, cultural amnesia, and injustice
continue to be long-running themes for this otherwise distinct
trio, while their settings and styles are constantly changing.
In *The Seventh Day*, Yu Hua built a novel around real-life news
stories that he exaggerated and set in the afterlife, among the
walking dead. A zombie woman adopts twenty-seven aborted
fetuses that had been discarded in a river as "medical refuse." A
migrant worker sells his kidney to buy his dead girlfriend a nice
burial plot. A man who was executed for his wife's murder discovers that she is still alive. For Yu Hua, contemporary society
is lost in an urban purgatory in which living is cheap, death is
expensive, and justice is fleeting.

Su Tong is best known for writing about unjust social hier-
archies in the Republican era, most famously in *Wives and Con-
cubines* (which was adapted by Zhang Yimou into the film *Raise
the Red Lantern*). But in his recent book, *Shadow of the Hunter*,
he also captures the madness and injustice that underpin contemporary China when truth and personal history are buried.
A strange young man is falsely accused and imprisoned for
rape, and whose grandfather, thinking he has lost his soul,

is institutionalized for digging up the streets in search of his ancestor's bones. Looking to the past for answers is a sure sign of insanity in the eyes of a society that either chooses to disregard the past, or edits it to suit their own ends.

In Ge Fei's award-winning Jiangnan trilogy, he goes back to the revolutionary upheavals of China's twentieth century to expose the ways utopian political ideology was consistently forgotten, and ultimately destroyed, by individual hypocrisy and venality. In fact, in Ge Fei's ficton, forgetfulness is both the problem and the solution in modern Chinese society. In one of his first short stories, villagers who wrongfully executed a doctor for a heinous crime he didn't commit, are reassured by an elder that "time will make people forget everything." In his more recent fiction, there are benefits to forgetting, and even disavowing, wider society altogether. In his 2012 novella "The Invisibility Cloak," a quiet, unambitious classical music lover's solution to external injustice and insanity is psychological self-sufficiency, a state Ge Fei likens positively to a cricket that lives, sings, and dies in a closed box. It's the only way to ensure that the absurdity of the modern world has no traction. "If you could just stop nitpicking and dissecting every little thing," says the eccentric audiophile, "if you could learn to keep one eye closed and one eye open, and quit worrying about everything and everybody, you might discover that life is actually pretty fucking beautiful, am I right?"

Can Xue, the only female writer in this chapter, doesn't just "keep one eye closed." Her work is totally detached from surface reality. Born in 1953 to a family severely persecuted during the

36   1957 anti-Rightist campaigns, Can Xue likens herself to a blind subterranean creature that spends all its time "industriously ploughing through the earth." There is no writer in contemporary China who has so comprehensively prioritized interiority over surface. Her fiction resembles an almost shamanistic journey that some have dubbed her "inner long march." When Cuilan, a widowed prostitute hoping to recover from a romance, visits her ancestral home in the countryside, she encounters people who speak like cicadas, send smoke signals to no one, and sit in trees to escape "the earth's clamor." Skipping the need for relevance or context, these eccentric behaviors convey Can Xue's profound and almost telepathic attentiveness to subconscious states. This is how she writes:

> As he spoke the sky was already growing light. Cuilan wondered how it could be daybreak when she had not slept yet. She saw her cousin squinting and staring ahead, so she looked, too, and saw through the mist the red fireballs rolling along. Was it really Wei Bo?
>
> When they went back into the house, her cousin said something disconnected, "From each according to his ability, to each according to his needs."
>
> His wife placed a big pot of congee and two smaller plates of pickled vegetables on the table, then sat down on a stool and cried. Her husband said, "She's reminded of her youth."

As with Joyce or Faulkner, the streams of consciousness, although packed with jewels, demand a tenacious reader. Both devotees and critics have likened reading her fiction to being

trapped in a dream—almost every sentence seems discon-
nected. But while we might feel lost, Can Xue presents characters who are anything but; they possess what she describes as
a hard-won "taut emotional logic." In her novel *Love in the New
Millennium*, a lothario voluntarily enters a detention center in
order to feel liberated; two women choose to become prosti-
tutes in a spa to escape work in a mind-numbing clothes factory; a married couple become estranged because they know
each other too well. Her characters not only become symbols
of society's corruption; they are also spiritually free. They are
individualists who have their own emotional coherence, as if the
way to truly have agency in her world is to abandon any notion
of cause and effect. Can Xue is a fiercely experimental autodi-
dact who is prone to talking about herself in the third person,
and her pen-name, "leftover snow," or snow that refuses to melt,
evokes appropriate tenacity. Her fiction, which has a small but
devoted following, is an interrogation of personal endurance,
and a rare glimpse into the lives of people who have found a
hard-won sense of peace. "They don't have our good fortune,"
says one woman to her friend watching young couples arguing
in a river, "they haven't become history yet. It takes suffering
and waiting."

The past becoming history is what many writers of the older
generation fear most; for them, the psychic weight of history is
exhausting, but essential, even if young readers are tired of their
writers grappling with the past. This generational and political
disconnect is parodied by Yan Lianke in *The Day the Sun Died*,
when a fourteen-year-old boy begs the fictional "Yan Lianke" to
stop writing books that "resembled deserted graves."

38   In the early days of the COVID-19 outbreak in Wuhan, Yan Lianke urged some of his creative writing students to be "the people who have graves in their hearts, with memories etched in them; the people who remember and can someday pass on these memories to our future generations." Literature is a place in which topics and ideas can be suppressed but not buried. It can explain why things feel too good to be true, why contemporary society feels disconcerting and uncanny. Yan believes that the same line of magical thinking that produced the Great Leap Forward's smelting campaigns in the 1950s also created the artificially low number of official COVID casualties in 2020. "While memories may not give us the power to change reality," he told his students in the aftermath of the outbreak, "it can at least raise a question in our hearts when a lie comes our way."

Three decades after it was first written, Yu Hua's once-banned 1992 novel, *To Live* (in which almost everyone dies) recently soared to the top of the fiction bestseller charts. In a peculiar twist, this deferred success was due, in part, to an online endorsement from singer, actor, and all-around teen-idol Jackson Yee, who Yu Hua publicly thanked before addressing the pop star's young fans. "You are a unique generation," he said. "You are in a period where the future has come and the past has not yet passed." They are poignant and optimistic words. The past isn't dead, the present is unclear, and the future is unfixed.

Reality Bites
Coming of Age and the Urban Dream

"Don't look back. Don't be weak. You have to make sacrifices
in order to have a great future. And sometimes you have to be
cruel to yourself."
—Lu Yao, *Life*

It's an all too familiar generational rift; parents give their child
what they never had, children fail to live up to their parents'
expectations. And in Chen Xiwo's short story "Pain," a mother
can't figure out where she went wrong or why her only child can't
see how lucky she is. "You think I'm really happy?" her daughter
replies. "I'm in pain, I've been in pain ever since I was born."

Chen is a controversial writer in China who regularly creates allegories critiquing aspects of Chinese society. "Pain" is a
disturbing and sad story about a child's psychosomatic illness,
a mental disorder that her mother concedes is how the child
copes with ever-growing societal ills. It captures both the con-
tempt and pity writers of an older generation such as Chen feel
for young people growing up in the confusion of a capitalistic

40   and undemocratic China. The unknown source of their suffering may in fact exacerbate it, a state he refers to sympathetically as "groundless rebellion."

Until recently, the hardships facing the first generation
to be born after China's economic reforms in the late seventies have been given short shrift. Compared with their parents
and grandparents, they've had it easy. These young people are
not hungry, they are not tilling the fields, they have access to
good education and medical care, and, thanks to the one-child
policy, they do not have to share resources or attention with
siblings. Having come of age at a time of unprecedented prosperity and opportunity, many have been spoiled and are referred
to as "little emperors," doted upon by their parents, kitted out in
designer labels, and free to think only about themselves.

No more so than the teen idol authors of the "post-80s"*
era who became the most potent symbols of their generation's
moral failings. They were seen as self-serving rebels without
any cause. Ditching the old socialist systems of literary production, these young upstarts wrote insouciant fiction in the first
person, successfully commodifying their youth, side-stepping
government-backed publishing channels, and proving that
you didn't need to ace the *gaokao*, China's incredibly stressful
two-day college exam, to hit the big time.

The way had already been paved by post-seventies female
authors such as Wei Hui who seemed to represent the worst
of capitalist vices. Her 1999 semi-autobiographical "glam-lit"
novel *Shanghai Baby* detailed passionate sex scenes with her

---

* In China, people born after 1980 are known as the "post-80s generation,"
those born after 1990 the "post-90s generation," and so on.

married Western lover, in contrast to cuddles with her impotent Chinese boyfriend, and she and others became known as "body-writers." *Shanghai Baby* was banned, burned in the streets, and became a bestseller: unwelcome proof that in China's new market economy, sex and controversy were great for business.

A similar formula worked for literary heartthrob and renaissance man Feng Tang, another post-seventies writer whose adolescent, trying-to-get-laid novels sparked a prolific writing career for which he states sexuality is his "trademark." Stroll in to any urban book shop and, after President Xi Jinping, Feng's smoldering profile picture is likely the second-most-common face on visible dustjackets. In 2016, his translation of the Indian poet Rabindranath Tagore's *Stray Birds* was pulled from bookshelves because Feng had re-translated "the world puts off its mask of vastness to its lover" to "the vast world opens the crotch of its trousers before its lover." Not the best choice of words perhaps, but the disproportionate outrage it provoked had all the markings of generational *schadenfreude*—petty proof that, as a writer and translator, Feng Tang was simply too big for his boots.

No two authors, however, have courted more criticism than Guo Jingming and Han Han, known as the "Janus face" of the more widely pilloried post-80s generation. They are to this day considered contemporary China's most galling success stories. Guo and Han were catapulted to fame as teenagers by their winning entries in the market-orientated New Concept Prize. Guo's unironic tales of Shanghai's vapid, wealthy youngsters, the so-called *baifumei* and *gaofushuai*—"white, rich beautiful girls" and "tall rich handsome boys"—foregrounded luxury and frivolity and earned him a reputation for writing shallow, commercial nonsense. The title of his fashionista trilogy, *Tiny Times,* became a byword for the era in which the grand, revolutionary themes of the past had been usurped by small, superficial concerns. In recent years, his novels such as *Cry Me a Sad River* have lost their fluffiness, dealing with subjects like bullying and suicide, a shift in tone that mirrors his own maligned status as a writer.

Han Han remains the unrivaled, unreconstructed king of controversy, however, whose light teen novels and combative blog won him millions of followers on Weibo, China's Twitter. In his twenties Han had an unprecedented level of individual influence, making it difficult for even the government to keep him under control. A handsome, cocky, clever high school dropout, his fearless and unflappable response to critics, sometimes on TV, made him a thrilling and dogged defender of his apparently apathetic, apolitical, historically nihilistic, self-centered generation:

> Those people in the past, they simply found themselves cared about *by* politics whether they liked it or not, and the roles they played were just that of small fry, hapless victims swept around in the political currents of the day. Being a victim is no decent topic of conversation, any more than being raped has a place in a proper range of sexual experiences. The era when one can care about politics has yet to arrive.

Thanks to his flagrant disregard for his elders and their politics, in a society once again increasingly shaped by Confucian values and social responsibility, Han Han was guaranteed to be a problematic role model. But his vocal repudiation of China's

rigid education system—often a byword for the government
itself—and all those parents who overstate its importance as a
path to success, emboldened his young audience to question the
pressures heaped upon them.

The fact that now, nearly in his forties, Han Han has abandoned fiction and intellectual fisticuffs to spend his time racing
expensive cars or writing screenplays about racing expensive
cars is, for some, gratifying proof that this firebrand turned
brand influencer was always nothing but a charlatan. "They are
not as rebellious or independent as we had thought," declared
novelist Yan Lianke, having hoped that Han Han's fighting spirit
might have matured into meaningful engagement. Even Han
Han's peers agree. "This is a failed generation," concluded the
young literary scholar Yang Qingxiang with a degree of personal
humility, in a now famous 2013 essay called "What Should the
Post-80s Do?". He described his generation as suspended and
ahistorical, a group without an identity and, as a literary critic,
argues that they "have produced no significant works of literature." In summary, "Post-80s" is no longer merely a descriptive
term but a pejorative label.

This generation did succeed, however, in drawing attention
to a noticeable void in Chinese culture. Literature about being
young in freshly built cities had not yet been written. Before
homegrown authors came around, young urban readers filled
the gap with offerings from Japan, including the magical, melancholic adventures of Murakami, the escapist mysteries of
Keigo Higashino, and with anime, comics, and games (ACG).
Author Zhou Jianing (another winner of the New Concept
Prize) believes that Murakami owes his popularity to having
"somehow maintained the status of a young person. This is

44   exactly what Chinese literature is missing." But this came with
its own burden. So much of the fiction written by the generation before them, the *zhiqing*—Mao's "sent-down youth"—
lamented their lost adolescence, when they were deprived of
schooling, romance, and sex. These formative years had been
sacrificed for the socialist ideals that were shattered under
Mao and forsaken by his successor, Deng Xiaoping. As a result,
the post-seventies and -eighties writers who wrote brazenly
about getting laid, going to university, and shopping seemed
tone-deaf, gratuitous, and entitled. They took it all for granted.

A public 2018 showdown between the poet Guo Lusheng,
a figurehead of the sent-down-youth generation, and a rela-
tively unknown young writer named Yu Xiuhua drew attention
to this generational fault line. Guo, who endured horrendous political persecution during the Cultural Revoltion and
whose 1968 poetry collection had once lamented the collective's humiliating annihilation of the individual under Mao,
condemned Yu's individualism: "How can a poet not spend a
moment considering the fate of humanity, or thinking about
the future of her nation?" he asked, directing his criticism specifically at Yu's apparently flippant desire for coffee, chats,
and sex in her poem "I Crossed Half of China to Sleep with
You." But her defiant counterattack online was characteristic
of a new voice in a competitive, socially stratified society. "My
fault," she said, "lies in being on the bottom rung of society and
yet still insisting on holding my head up high." Yu's lust for life
represented a way for young people, especially those on "the
bottom rung," to change their fate. It's a front-footed individualism that continues to offend the taste of some of the older
generations.

Rather than focusing on their own desires, hardships, and failures, Yan Lianke echoed various intellectuals of his generation by suggesting educated young urban authors *should* have instead been writing about their migrant worker peers, for whom the relentless struggle to change one's fate has been so much harder. The movement of people from countryside to town has occurred on a mythic scale in the post-Reform era, creating a new subaltern—or "bottom rung"—class. An estimated 300 million rural migrant workers have been living in towns and cities without the same rights as those with urban residency. Many effectively live as illegal immigrants in their own country, having travelled to an emerald city that keeps its gate closed.

A muddling array of pejorative terms are used to describe them, and illustrates just how casually they've been used and discarded: "vagrants," "the floating population," "workers for the boss," "low-end population," "i slaves"—the list goes on. In 2002, a novel by You Fengwei called *Loach*, titled after the bottom-feeding fish, followed three young male migrants who have moved to the city to make their fortunes. The city ends up crushing their futures: one is forced into prostitution and executed, another is accidentally castrated. Early in the book, they look up at a writer's window in a high-rise apartment:

"What should we do to make him see us?" one of them asks.
"Wave at him."
"He can't see."
"Shout at him."
"He can't hear."
"Then, there is only one way."

"What?'
        "Burn ourselves so that we shine like lamps."

The novel belongs to an important and already established literary genre in China known as "bottom rung" or "subaltern" fiction (*diceng wenxue*). It is a continuation of a powerful literary diktat that came out of the May Fourth Movement of the 1920s, that fiction must have a clear moral and social function. Literature should "flip minds" (*fanxin*) and awaken readers to the suffering of those less fortunate—and in so doing, inspire change and resistance.

However, one of the most significant literary breakthroughs in post-Reform China is that rural migrant workers no longer need middle-class writers in high-rise apartments to tell their story for them—they are writing it themselves. The easy internet access that has overlapped with China's industrialization has given migrant writers a means of publication unprecedented in the global history of "worker literature" and, in particular, the most comprehensive migrant worker poetry movement in the world.

In 2017 a domestic worker's diary, "I am Fan Yusu," went viral in China. Fan lamented the hours spent raising someone else's children while being away from her own. An estimated 69 million "left-behind children" remain in their rural hometowns, being raised by extended family. Parents often only manage to return once a year, for the Spring Festival, the break following the Chinese New Year. Miner Chen Nianxi juxtaposes the tiny gains yielded by his work underground with the vast expanse his job puts between him and his son:

your dad is tired
each step is only three inches wide
and three inches take a year
son, use your math to calculate
how far your dad can go

Just a few words convey a plaintive hope that his son's math is good enough to calculate his father's sacrifice, as well as his own attempt to educate his son while toiling down a pit.

The most famous of the migrant poets is Xu Lizhi, who in 2014, when he was only twenty-four years old, threw himself off the seventeenth floor of a mall across the road from his favorite book shop. He had worked at the Foxconn factory in Shenzhen, known for making all of our Apple products. In 2010 Foxconn had responded to an increase in attempted suicides among workers by erecting nets to prevent deaths, rather than considering why there was a need for them. A fellow worker wrote: "To die is the only way to testify that we ever lived." But with or without his death, Xu's poetry managed to expose the sinister myth of opportunity and social mobility that underwrites a life on the production line and implicates the whole society:

I swallowed an iron moon
they called it a screw

I swallowed industrial wastewater and
    unemployment forms
bent over machines, our youth died young,

48
> I swallowed labor, I swallowed poverty
> swallowed pedestrian bridges, swallowed this
>> rusted-out life
>
> I can't swallow any more
> everything I've swallowed roils up in my throat
>
> I spread across my country
> a poem of shame

While the post-80s writers are known for their self-confidence, the poetry of migrant workers is characterized by self-sacrifice. To live in the city, they literally risk life and limb. Poet Xie Xiangnan dispassionately describes how a twenty-year-old female worker severs her finger at the end of a twelve-hour shift:

> people reported after it happened she
> didn't cry and didn't
> scream she just grabbed her finger
> and left

Xie was also an assembly worker himself: "My finest five years went into the input feeder of a machine," he writes. "I watched those five youthful years come out of the machine's asshole—each formed into an elliptical plastic toy."

A few female migrants have used fiction to actively challenge the widespread, unspoken assumptions that migrant women's bodies are available for other kinds of consumption. Novelist Sheng Keyi was a migrant worker who, like the

female protagonist Qian Xiaohong ("Little Red") in her debut
novel, *Northern Girls*, left rural Hunan to find work in metropolitan Shenzhen. The novel explores the pursuit of sexual
autonomy—having lots of sex but never for money—as a way
to overcome the pernicious stigma of the female migrant as a
prostitute. However, in a surreal twist, Little Red's huge breasts
won't stop growing, proof of how difficult it is for a female
migrant worker to insist that her value is not merely sexual,
even if she ultimately succeeds in changing her life on her own
terms. But Sheng was in fact able to make a rare, hard-won leap
from migrant worker to literary star, going on to write, among
many others, *The Metaphor Detox Centre* and *Death Fugue*, both
banned on the mainland for her depiction of reality as a carefully manipulated dystopia.

Unfortunately, for writers such as Xu Lizhi, the tragedy
of his death was that it seemed to prove that poetry couldn't
change his life after all—as if becoming successful would have
been the only measure of his poetry's value. His poor, elderly
father, devastated by his son's death, didn't know his son wrote
poetry until after he died. "It can't compare with science and
technology," his father said. "Poetry was important in dynastic
times, when it was part of the civil service exam . . . you could be
an official if you wrote good poetry. But society has changed a
lot. It's not that I don't support him, but in today's world, if you
don't have money or power, it's really hard."

The forgivable pragmatism of the older generation, like Xu's
father, is depicted in post-90s writer Qian Jianan's impressive debut novel *No Eggs for Them* as being akin to frogs sitting
in water that is slowly being brought to boil, expecting young

50   people to do the same: work hard, marry, try to make money while you can. This era of economic uplift, the older generation fears, can't be forsaken for poetry, art, or literature. Coincidentally, there's a scene in *The Continent*, a movie written by Han Han, in which two friends joke about frogs in boiling pans. "They'll jump out. That's what happens in reality," says one, before his friend slams a lid on the pot, declaring: "Now this is reality."

This kind of cynicism is unwelcome within established literary circles in which an older generation of critics are keen to promote young writers who create a more considerate, class-conscious, social-realist fiction, one that is more aligned with their own literary heritage. Zhang Yueran, considered a beacon within the "failed generation," depicts young urbanites with a social, rather than individual, conscience. In her story, "Home," a young couple simultaneously leave each other, their apartment, and urban life, unaware that they're perfectly in sync. They leave their empty home to their cleaner, a migrant worker who had fled an abusive marriage, and who now has the time and space to finally consider her own dreams. The event uniting all three characters is the 2008 earthquake in Sichuan, which is the migrant cleaner's home province, and the place to which the couple fled, to assist in the relief effort. The disaster killed at least 70,000 people and inspired a massive national effort to help those affected, and is often seen as a watershed moment in which young people woke up to the suffering of their fellow citizens. Zhang Yueran's perfectly formed story reads like a contemporary take on Lu Xun's "literature as vehicle for moral message."

Taking up the mantle of writers who came before them
has made several younger authors more aware of the distance
between the generations, and the pressure to reconnect them.
The paternalism of the literary world, the inbuilt respect for
elders in all Confucian societies, now compounded by an aging
society, in which a third of the population will be over the age of
sixty by 2050, might explain why many are not writing about
being young in the city, but instead about old people who have
failed to adapt to it. Screenwriter and novelist Shuang Xuetao
writes with his delightfully ironic and chatty metropolitan tone
about aging men who are heroes in their field—a chess maestro,
a proud foreman—who have lost their place and meaning in
modern society. A postman in Lu Min's "Xie Bomao RIP" wastes
his dying years fruitlessly trying to deliver letters sent to an
imaginary recipient—a neat metaphor for the obsolescence felt
by many older people in the city.

Elderly outsiders populate post-90s writer Wang Zhanhei's two short story collections, *Air Cannon* and *Neighborhood
Adventures*: a firecracker dealer who's adrift during Chinese
New Year, now that anti-pollution laws have put him out of
business; a grandmother who's rejected by her money-grubbing
son and turns to communing with people's rubbish. They are
powerful, if occasionally sentimental, vignettes that in 2018
won Wang Zhanhei the inaugural Blancpain-Imaginist Award,
established to celebrate specifically noncommercial fiction by
writers under forty-five. The judging panel, which included Yan
Lianke, praised the post-90s writer's use of realism to depict
the lives of ordinary urban people, which perhaps doubles as a
backhanded criticism of the generation that preceded her. The

52   post-80s writers have become a cautionary tale of what not to write about—themselves.

For those who do write about their own experiences, their work often internalizes—or parodies—the ways in which focusing on (and even writing about) oneself is considered the root cause of failure. Young, melancholic poets lament not just poetry as a poor career choice, but their corresponding inability to be a somebody—a tricky ambition in which status is often gauged by the intentionally vague concept of *suzhi*, or "quality." Informed by society's complex value judgments, writers such as Fu Yuehui and Zhou Jianing deploy self-consciously cruel and inscrutable narrators to critique themselves and others jockeying for small, social advantages. And at a time when diligence and hard work are part of the government's national project, indolence is the most rebellious act of all. From Lu Nei's Salingeresque fuck-ups to the funny, feckless dossers in stories by Da Tou Ma and Wu Qing, many authors born in the last three decades have embraced a lack of drive with a mixture of humility, inevitability, and comedic pride—an irreverence that has recently transformed itself into a growing countercultural movement widely known as "lying flat" or *tangping*—consciously opting out of the rat race.

Having come of age at the same time as China's contemporary cities, most people born in the seventies and eighties belong to the first one-child, urban, globalized generation in China. With the iron rice bowl long gone, theirs is a time of stark differences in opportunities for those with rural or urban residence cards (*hukou*), between rich and poor, between old and young, while the shift from the collective to the individual has shattered the notion of communal experience. They are a frontier

generation whose apparent mistakes and failures should be seen
as the forgivable result of growing up in uncharted territory.

There is one writer who is still treasured by both young and old, rich and poor, cynical and optimistic. Lu Yao, who in 1991 was awarded the Mao Dun Literature Prize, chronicled poor, rural idealists dreaming of a new life in the city at the very start of Reform and Opening Up. Although he died in 1992, before most of his current readers were even born, Lu's enduring success can be boiled down to the enormous sympathy he has for the young characters in his novels who tried to change their fate, and failed. Forty years on, his books *Life* and *Ordinary World* continue to offer consolation for a new generation who haven't achieved what they or their parents hoped for. Nevertheless, in China's increasingly competitive and stratified urban society, it turns out that bombastic, failsafe fantasies of omnipotence and wealth offer the greatest comfort of all.

The Factory
The Business of Online Escapism

"Before any of the legends of the business world have risen,
  I will be the first, eternal legend!"
  —*Extraordinary Genius*, by Poor Four

"Once my profound veins are fixed, a sleeping dragon will be
  awakened from the abyss. I will make those people who look
  down on me and those who think that the Xia Clan took in a
  wastrel for their son-in-law obediently shut their traps."
  —*Against the Gods*, by Mars Gravity

Self-serving, shameless, and status-obsessed, the borderline
sociopathic heroes in many of China's hugely popular online
fantasy novels have captivated young readers and become a nig-
gling problem for the Party. Not because these often silly, endless sagas are in fact searing parodies of people in high places,
but rather that the millions of online novels that are being
churned out seem proof that, despite government narratives

emphasizing core socialist values, mainstream culture is gov-   55
erned by the mercenary, amoral instincts of the market.

China may have only embraced aspects of capitalism in
the last forty years or so, but the mainland's internet literature
boom makes it the largest self-generating industry of unregu-
lated, free-market fiction in the world. Novels live or die based
purely on the number of readers they attract and hold on to. And
President Xi is not a fan. In 2014, he launched a series of attacks
on China's already swollen web-novel industry, dubbing it a
"plateau without summits." He condemned its widespread pla-
giarism and warned artists to neither "lose themselves in the
tide of market economy" nor let their work carry "the stench of
money." But this is a cultural phenomenon that has thrived on
the CCP's watch. It is the mutant offspring of societal and cultural strictures, and unrestrained economic growth. If the first
flush of the internet in China was a place of literary experimen-
tation and bold social critique, by 2002 it was mainly a source
of copyright infringements and self-published escapist YA fiction that, while not encouraged, was left to multiply. And multiply. And multiply.

While Americans are no strangers to online fan fiction,
Twitter thread thrillers, and even niche hypertext "novels,"
nothing compares to the sheer scale of Chinese web fiction.
Today, online reading platforms are crammed with more than
24 million fiction titles by writers who, depending on their
stamina, hammer out between 3,000 and 30,000 words every
day, hoping to catch and keep the "eyeballs" of 430 million
currently active readers. Consumers devote hours on end to
devouring daily updates through reading apps on their mobile

56   phones. Many use a pay-per-view or monthly subscription to
      unlock later chapters. Any profits are shared with the platform
      hosts, of which China Literature is now the biggest. Just as users
      weaned on social media expect a perpetually refreshed news-
      feed, this literature is produced and consumed in the same way:
      Dickens-style serialization for the TikTok era.

      Despite Xi's understandable misgivings, those with most to
      gain from the industry—the cultural industrialists themselves,
      such as (former) co-chief executive of China Literature Wu
      Wenhui—are keen to celebrate Chinese web fiction as one of the
      four "cultural wonders of the world," after Hollywood, Korean
      idol dramas, and Japanese anime. It's touted as China's most
      realistic shot at exerting cultural soft power, with web novels
      becoming an unlikely success story abroad on platforms such as
      WuxiaWorld and WebNovel, the international version of one of
      China's largest reading platforms, Qidian.

      Last year a Californian named Kevin Cazad credited a Chi-
      nese web novel called *Coiling Dragon* with miraculously curing
      his cocaine addiction. The novel, written by one of China's
      richest writers, I Eat Tomatoes (to fans, just Tomato), is a fusion
      of Eastern and Western fantasy (a genre known as *xuanhuan*),
      that charts the rise and rise of Linley Baruch, a member of the
      once formidable Dragonblood clan. In order to restore the clan
      to its former glory, Linley cultivates his *qi* (a power source stored
      just beneath the navel) as he battles up the pecking order from
      lowly warrior to Universe Creator. Thrilled by Cazad's rehabil-
      itation from drug addiction, some Chinese media outlets were
      quick to hail the health benefits of Chinese web fiction in gen-
      eral. "Chinese online novels are the first shot made by any

culture worldwide to stop drug addiction," declared one news
organization.

It seems more likely, however, that Cazad simply swapped
one narcotic for another. Owing to their addictive quality and
short-term thrills, domestic readers dub web fiction *yiyin,* or
"YY" for short, meaning "lust of the mind" or "lust of intent."
The concept itself has literary origins, appearing for the first
time in Cao Xueqin's 1792 vernacular novel *Dream of the Red
Chamber* as a way of exploring the connection between one's fantasies and real-life events. In modern parlance, however, YY has
lost its philosophical sheen and instead evokes something more
like "mental porn," a guilty pleasure that offers short-term highs,
long-term dependency, and even physical debasement. Starting
to read a story that is still unfinished is known as "jumping into a
hole," waiting for the latest update is "squatting" in one.

The pitfalls, and pleasures, of escapism are nothing new. At the
turn of the twentieth century, a fluffy genre known as Mandarin
Ducks and Butterflies—named after the birds that are mostly
seen in pairs, and the classic *Butterfly Lovers,* a tragic folktale of
thwarted love—was extremely popular. Rooted in gossip and
lacking any didactic social agenda, these pulpy romances were
denounced by writers of the May Fourth Movement, who prioritized realism, science, and moral purpose. Among that movement's most revered alumni was Lu Xun, whose novella *The
True Story of Ah Q,* about a man in a blissful state of ignorance, is
used to this day to criticize social and artistic apathy. An "Ah Q
mentality" means any self-deluded soul who refuses to face up
to reality.

58   The hyperreality of *wuxia,* China's most enduring escapist genre, has always been embedded with weightier political allegories. It's thought to stretch back 2,000 years, concerning a mythical world of martial arts heroes (now associated in the West with films such as *Crouching Tiger, Hidden Dragon,* based on a classic *wuxia* novel) that offers an idealized, rival code of ethics. *Wuxia* revolves around renegade knights-errant, a group of superior martial artists who live in a world of clans known as the *jianghu,* many of whom hold corrupt imperial courts to account, defend their sect, or seek vengeance for a slain master. During the twentieth century, the genre fell out of favor with both the Nationalists and the Communists, precisely because outsiders challenging corrupt courts seemed a fantasy a little too near the knuckle.

In fact, Mao placed a blanket ban on all commercial genre fiction because, naturally, there was no crime in socialist China, no need for fantasy when society defers to science, and no use for romance when one loved the Party above all else. With Mao's death, however, genre fiction got a new lease on life. Novelist Zhang Jie rekindled romance as a topic in 1980 with her controversial short story "Love Must Not Be Forgotten," about a female cadre who never acted upon her feelings. And the bewitching 1950s- and 1960s-era *wuxia* novels by Jin Yong, written in Hong Kong and banned on the mainland until 1984, reignited a thirst for escapist novels about chivalry and camaraderie that was later quenched by Japanese ACG culture.

However, Chinese internet fiction today, having evolved quickly and virulently, often depicts a fantasy world not of camaraderie but of brute individualism. They are fantasies that are escapist in detail but familiar in spirit to the world the readers and writers inhabit. All consumer societies require the illusion of new styles to sell products, and, despite a deceptively diverse range of genres and subgenres,* if one is to generalize millions of these titles, especially those split along wearisome gender lines, Chinese web novels cater to young men longing to become a successful tycoon or supreme godlike warrior—and to young women longing to bewitch him.

"Male-oriented titles" (of which Qidian, owned by China Literature, is by far the dominant platform) are less likely to be adapted for TV and are snapped up by gaming, anime, and manga industries. This is in part due to the fact that a "shame-less" main character (MC) has become the clichéd way to sep-arate Chinese from, say, Japanese and Korean light novels. The hero is an unreconstructed embodiment of toxic masculinity known in China as "straight man cancer."

These mendacious, vengeful, overpowered, harem-building, individualistic hotheads will stop at nothing to become the most powerful being—or businessman. Shameless heroes excel at "face-slapping," the intentional humiliation of opponents that has almost become a genre in itself. In a society where the concept of "face," or respect and social standing, are still

---

* Categories on platforms such as 17K, Zhongheng, Jinjiang Literature City, and Qidian include: eastern fantasy; immortal hero; martial arts; urban; science fiction; military; gaming; sports; history; ancient romance; modern romance; fairy-tale; young romance; fantasy romance. The ever-expanding, unofficial subgenres include: tomb-raiding; feudal lord; magic campus; apocalypse; native village; hot-blooded youth; career battle; fabricated history; ROC Reminiscence (Republic of China 1912–1949); career beauty; gaming love.

60 of huge importance, the defeat and embarrassment of a nemesis is a vicarious thrill for many readers. Their heroes might be Yun Che, in *Against the Gods*, who smites everyone (and I mean everyone) who looks down on him. Or Yi Yun, in *True Martial World*, who demeans his defeated enemies by threatening to kill them with a brick. Or in the "real world" of business, a washed-up twenty-seven-year-old investor from the modern day is reborn in the early eighties at the start of Reform and Opening Up, and uses his *Back to the Future* foresight to become the richest man in the world. The story, called *Extraordinary Genius*, might be more aptly titled *Lucky Asshole*.

Most shameless MCs have become synonymous with *xianxia*, a genre also known as "cultivation" or "immortal hero," which typically follows a young low-status male repeatedly "leveling-up" to become the supreme being in that particular multiverse. In Er Gen's hugely popular *I Shall Seal the Heavens*, failed scholar Meng Hao is kidnapped and taken to live with the Reliance Sect, a society that rejects Confucian ethics and worships the laws of the jungle instead. Meng Hao adapts to the new dog-eat-dog world with gusto. By about a quarter of the way through the novel, which is about 300 chapters in, Meng Hao has embraced a survival-of-the-fittest mentality, turned himself into a despicable swindler, cheated people and beasts to accrue wealth (spirit stones and immortal jades), and vanquished countless opponents on his path to supremacy. Mercy is for wimps.

It's worth mentioning, however, that these absurd antiheroes can be really funny, intentionally or otherwise, as a source of genuine comedy for readers, who love the repetitive reminders of incomparable looks (ageless jadelike skin, eyes like stars) and unmatchable abilities (supreme intelligence, wit, strength, and sexual irresistibility), all filtered through the personality of a narcissistic baby. Some might be turned off by such buffoonery, but living (and floundering) in an era of perceived social Darwinism, younger readers clearly appreciate the satire at its heart. It says less about their own "shamelessness" and more about the society in which they struggle to get ahead.

Online platforms have offered women unprecedented opportunities to write and publish their own work in an industry that has been largely dominated by men. Nevertheless, while romance narratives that make up most of the "female-orientated" titles are generally less toxic than "male-orientated" fantasies, they are just as unreconstructed. Stories revolve around idealized girls-next-door who become the sole inamorata of a high-status bachelor or demigod. Again, it's nothing that Western readers wouldn't already recognize. The narratives still revolve around attracting male attention. More than seventy years after Chairman Mao declared that "women hold up half the sky" and criminalized arranged marriages, prostitution, child betrothal, and concubinage, young romance writers seem to go out their way to repeal equality for the purposes of storytelling.

A patriarchal dynamic is baked into innumerable palace romances, in which a modern female protagonist reincarnates as a concubine or a servant girl in ancient times. Her feisty and free-thinking twenty-first-century personality attracts the jealousy of her rivals, and inflames the passions of the powerful man she loves—who owns or controls her.

Novels set in contemporary times often feature romance that is even more transactional. The story might start with the female lead agreeing to sign a contract to a loveless marriage,

62   as she does in *My Dangerous Billionaire Husband* and *Trial Mar-riage Husband: Need to Work Hard*. Or she might enter into a sur-rogacy service for a wealthy CEO, as in *One Birth Two Treasures: The Billionaire's Sweet Love*. These romances are built around exploitive, mercenary arrangements that slowly start to simmer. Girls are willing to overlook the abusive characteristics of a suc-cessful man as soon as she becomes the only girl he wants.

Perhaps it is no surprise that professional success rep-resents a fantasy for many young Chinese readers. The majority are under twenty-five, some young enough to still be immersed in or reeling from the pressures of the *gaokao*. Others are strug-gling to enter the competitive world of the workplace. Com-monly referred to, including by themselves, as *diaosi* (variously translated as "penis hairs," "dick shreds," or "losers"), this cap-tive group of young readers are often comically aware of the stark contrast between the superheroes they read about and their own perceived insignificance.

And these online communities often take ironic pride in it. Incredibly active forums that host communities of young readers commenting on each and every sentence mean that reading online fiction is by no means a passive or private hobby. Novels that don't retain enough likes and shares have their contracts canceled. Authors seeking high approval rat-ings must incorporate endless reader feedback, creating a vast echo chamber of "prosumers"—producers and consumers—replicating the competitive wider world they seek to both con-quer and escape. Much like the corrupt and cutthroat business model of the online influencer, writers regularly self-publicize, cozy up to readers, buy clicks, and offer "red packet" donations to boost ratings.

Given that online novels live or die according to their popularity metrics, they have acquired distinctive algorithmic traits.
First, size matters. "The novel's ranking, influence, and author's
fame are all affected by the novel's length," says Qidian. Owing to
a pay-per-view system, and one that only kicks in after the first
100 chapters, novels are often more than 6 million words long,
making both reading and writing a Sisyphean task. Second, in
order to keep readers hooked over thousands of chapters, narratives are structured like computer games. A vast, geeky hier-
archy of levels, cheats, treasures, and magical objects create the
constant illusion of progress.

Finally, as is also the case in some Japanese and Korean
light novels, the main character is almost always reborn within
the first few chapters. It's unclear whether it was originally
inspired by the fluid number of lives given in computer games,
the Buddhist concept of reincarnation, or an unspoken emotional desire for a new start in life, but the fantasy is a gift to
a lowly protagonist who might carry over memories, skills,
and powerful objects from a previous life, to exact revenge and
cultivate status or allure. This kind of reincarnation sets up a
groundless world in which actions are without organic origin
or just consequence—the exact opposite to a coming-of-age
tale. Online characters don't change anything but their circum-
stances and status.

Take Er Gen's *I Shall Seal the Heavens.* After 1,614 chapters,
Meng Hao has lived for 3 billion years, cultivated his *qi* from
lowly mortal to Supreme Entity of the Vast Expanse, and has
transcended the passage of time itself. And yet, in the end, he
can't resist destroying a foolish young cultivator who makes
a naïve power grab, killing him *and* eliminating him from the

memory of all who knew him. He has optimized his power but lost none of his pettiness.

Lack of character development and moral maturity is almost certainly a by-product of the speed with which these novels are produced. Many of the most impressively prolific writers churn out 20,000 to 30,000 words a day (the length of this book), a process that is by necessity knee-jerk and nonstop, requiring characters that are all action and no reflection. No wonder that the protagonists aren't finding the time to work on their social skills—the writers, working in thankless jobs by day and writing by night, aren't either.

Although writers are encouraged to see online fiction as a concrete path to fulfilling their dreams, only a few, like Tang Jia San Shao (aka Zhang Wei), live to tell the fairy tale. He may be one of China's wealthiest writers, earning $18 million in 2017 alone. When asked about his own dreams as a writer, he said: "I want to influence the world with China's intellectual property . . . to build the 'Disney World of China'—a commercial real estate development with a theme park based on my stories at its center."

Online literature is often considered a business before an art form. Tang Jia San Shao's success gives hope to writers—protagonists cultivate *qi* as the author cultivates IP, intellectual property. But the sad irony for many online authors is that they find themselves re-creating the conditions of the factory, chained to their computers, hammering out thousands of words each night after work, manning virtual production lines in which supply can't meet demand. And, like manual workers in many other industries, many jobs may soon be destroyed by automation.

Cai Xiang, one of China's leading literary critics, makes the distinction between the "cultural bourgeoisie," who convert culture into capital, and the "cultural proletariat" or "intellectual laborer," who convert culture into labor. The dizzying success of Tang Jia San Shao remains a fantasy for the vast majority of online "writing hands." Like migrant workers, they dream of changing their destiny on a production line, when in reality cultural industrialists are simply cashing in.

The unironic motto of China Literature, subsidiary of the world's largest gaming and social media company, Tencent, is: "Live your dreams, don't waste your youth."* It's accompanied by a picture of a man riding a horse on a beach at sunset. Echoing its business-savvy star writers, China Literature introduces itself as "the leading digital reading platform and literature IP cultivation platform." They dangle the possibility of lucrative TV, film, and ACG adaptations, of which there have been an enticing amount, as golden carrots to incentivize millions of writers to join the assembly line. "Help readers to fantasize about what they lack," instructs Qidian's writing guide, an unashamedly cynical business strategy. Much like American self-help gurus, online literature platforms exploit people's thirst for success, enabling them to run formulaic fiction farms whose products—the novels—and whose producers—the

---

* This is, in part, a quote from a well-known poem called "Motherland" by one of China's most famous poets Hai Zi, who died by suicide at twenty-five in 1989. "Live your dreams" is more directly translated as "dreams as horses" to which China Literature then added "don't waste your youth."

66   writers—carry all the scars of being grown under the robotic
       glare of metrics and data. Writers live and work with machines,
       and are expected to perform like them. "I am not as capable as
       others," said one online author. "They can write up to 10,000
       or even 20,000 words per day while I can only write 4,000 to
       5,000. How should I punish myself?"

       In 2020, writers on the China Literature platform refused
       to update their novels after a sweeping change to the terms
       and conditions of their writing contracts. The founding mem-
       bers of China Literature had been replaced by executives from
       Tencent, and with the regime change came some face-slapping
       tweaks. With a push toward a free-to-view model, their already
       meager income would be taken away, writers would lose con-
       trol over their social media accounts, and China Literature
       would own the rights to their work until fifty years after their
       deaths, rendering their precious IP completely worthless. "This
       feels worse than being sold into slavery," said one writer. "This
       is class struggle," said another. "The bourgeoisie and capitalists
       only pursue profits, their pores ooze dirty blood, they squeeze
       the proletariat for every drop of oil they can." Although the dis-
       pute was eventually resolved, for writers taking aim at bour-
       geois capitalism, socialism hasn't been too kind either.

       Websites are increasingly required to undergo "internet
       cleansing," incorporating machine and manual censors to "rec-
       tify" their content, leaving thousands of novels locked. In a
       sudden bid for regulation, the government has imposed rating
       systems, not according to age or popularity, but based on how
       well the content scores on socialist values. Low scores require
       the whole website to be "rectified." Jinjiang Literature City, the
       most popular romance-focused platform, had to introduce a

manual censorship system in which readers earned points by
checking novels for political or sexual content, before the site
closed for a couple of weeks to machine-check 20 million chapters. Qidian went through a similar cull. Many books are still
locked, with no hope of the writers being granted access to their
own work.

One writer, who goes by the name of Tiaowu (which means
"dancing"), had racked up 7 million readers when whole chunks
of his novels were deleted. He tried incorporating tweaks—
no fights, no religion, no lesbians—but his work kept on being
deleted. "You can cut off the leaves, you can cut off the branches,
and the tree will live," he said. "But they had me fucking cut off
the entire fucking trunk." He said he had no choice but to stop
writing.

Further censorship and interference seems inescapable.
Despite its mounting appeal at home and abroad, online fiction's popularity might finally be its downfall. Where a lack
of eyeballs used to be the problem, now the issue for most
novels is that they might get too many, which, from the government's point of view, makes popular online fiction too hard
to regulate.

Right now, there are a plethora of state-approved writing
courses and opportunities, many of which gently push young
writers in the direction of realism and propaganda, urging them
to, somewhat ironically, make fantastical claims about historical heroes and martyrs. "Heroic figures that save the world and
humanity, as created in the work of many internet writers, are
in essence or spiritually the same as the heroes in red stories,"
said the deputy general of the Shanghai Writers Association,
Xue Shu, in the state-backed *Global Times*. He calls it "spiritual

68   sublimation." The most famous of these ordinary heroes is the model soldier Lei Feng, who died in 1962. While his existence is not disputed, his legacy is viewed with a mix of ridicule and reverence. The diary he supposedly left behind, chronicling his selfless devotion to the people, to Mao, and to the Party, is widely believed to be a complete work of fiction, commissioned as part of a propaganda campaign to "live Lei Feng." His role in the CCP pantheon amounts to a canonization.

The CCP is exerting a renewed drive to see its saints and martyrs appear in fiction. In 2021, the Shanghai Writers Association commissioned stories from its "Red Footprints" program to celebrate the centenary of the founding of the Party, a project set up for young internet writers to spread "red culture." In a strange twist, a movement called "Little Pinks," a reference to a discussion forum on Jinjiang Literature City's website, has become synonymous with a rise in online nationalism (even though there is little evidence that young female romance readers double up as patriotic vigilantes), a group that the government wishes to both harness and tamp down. Tang Jia San Shao's latest novel, *Medial Axis of Beijing*, about a cultural relic restorer, was supposedly written to support an official application for a 7.8-kilometer stretch of the capital to be classified as a UNESCO World Heritage Site. In keeping with government directives, he apparently now wants to focus less on fantasy, and more on realism.

The government has even established its own authorized version of the web novel industry, the world's inaugural University of Online Fiction, which hopes to attract 100,000 students a year. Mo Yan is nominally at the helm, a move he finds as peculiar as anyone else: "I did not expect to be honorary president," he said. The university's stated aims are to "fully implement the party's educational policy, take the concept of scientific development as the guide, follow the laws of education, make the cultivation of talent the foundation, let the establishment of academic rigor lead the way, take the 'Chinese Dream' as the spiritual guide, make the continuation of Chinese culture one's duty, pursue the harmonious unity of scientific and humanistic values, adhere to the concept that 'creativity changes life,' and to run a non-profit vocational educational university that will serve Chinese people around the world who love online literature."

Being forced to write within such bureaucratic and turgid guidelines suddenly casts the strange world of online fiction in a more sympathetic light. It's enough to make you long to read about petty narcissistic supermen, and root for the plucky, powerless writers who were compelled to create them in the first place.

Pushing Boundaries

Alternative Comics, Boys' Love, and Ethnic Borderlands

"People keep silent for any number of reasons, some because
they lack the ability or opportunity to speak, others because
they are hiding something, and still others because they feel,
for whatever reason, a certain distaste for the world of speech."
—Wang Xiaobo, *The Silent Majority*

Bill Clinton's suggestion back in 2000 that the internet would
bring democracy to China and that trying to control it would
be like "nailing Jell-O to the wall" seems pretty comical these
days. The spread of online disinformation in the US and UK is
now almost certainly the greatest threat to Western democracy, while the CCP has the Jell-O exactly where it wants it:
The internet is the government's most effective tool of surveillance and suppression. Dystopian science fiction has long predicted this misapplication of technology, with Chinese science
fiction writers Han Song, Ma Boyong, and Zhang Ran all imagining the chilling ways in which technology can imperceptibly
change reality—machines that harmonize people and objects

at an atomic level, ear pieces that edit out "unhealthy" ideas or atmospheric nanobots used to bowdlerize all information. The nature of truth has shifted in the digital age, and the only solution offered in these stories is to go offline and off grid.

However, online agitators in China, committed to temporary acts of rebellion, have made specific use of the Chinese language to stay under the radar. Chinese, with its tones and the logographic structure of its characters, is an exceptionally adaptable language for censorship-skirting puns. Ai Weiwei's art installation of 3,000 porcelain river crabs paid tribute to the cheeky wordplay that had been swirling online ever since then-president Hu Jintao launched his concept of a "harmonious society." "River crab" and "harmony" in Chinese are homophones (*hexie*): To be "river-crabbed" meant to be censored or rectified.

The imagistic quality of Chinese characters enabled them to be repurposed in the captivating, if now largely defunct, world of "Martian language," which involved splitting and splicing individual characters to create new ones to avoid censorship. "Human rights人权" was instead written as "人木又"—the word "rights 权" split into its component parts, 木 and 又.

By extension, images have become some of the most effective modes of dissent for online rebels in recent years, as they are much harder for inhuman algorithms to search and censor. Politically subversive content, known as black or *hei* material, requires subtlety behind the great firewall. Political cartoonist Kuang Biao is most famous for his picture of the silenced Wuhan whistleblower doctor Li Wenliang wearing a barbed-wire face mask. Wang Liming, aka Rebel Pepper, was forced into exile in Japan and America, offering a safer distance for him to portray President Xi—who can't be mocked or critiqued inside

72 China—with his head resembling a bright red, swollen coronavirus molecule.

China has become the biggest comic book market in the
world, but it's dominated by Japanese manga, many of which
have been blacklisted by the CCP in recent years on the grounds
that they "include scenes of violence, pornography, terrorism
and crimes against public morality." But despite the best
efforts of the Communist Youth League to launch homegrown
and state-friendly alternatives on its own online ACG Bilibili
channel (the most notable being *The Leader*, about the life of
Karl Marx), the Japanese manga industry is a juggernaut that
can't be stopped.

At the fringes, however, China has its own independent and
underground comics scene. It represents a small, liminal community of artists who have elevated the mundanities of everyday
life to tragi-comic extremes. Populated with misshapen misfits,
oddballs, slobs, lonely middle-aged men, undignified youths, and
endearingly charmless nonconformists, these comics are drawn
and written in a style that is intentionally scratchy and slipshod.

Production-wise, work is shared online via private and
public groups. But crucially, they are also self-published in
exciting, limited editions. They are often dinky, palm-sized,
serialized, single-frame images, in the tradition of *lianhuanhua*,
picture storybooks that emerged in China at the start of the
twentieth century. They can often only be found in discreet,
by-appointment-only outlets, or printed on demand in the
artists' residential studios. The earliest print editions of Special Comix, a limited-edition compilation series showcasing
some of the most active and exciting comic artists, are much
sought-after collector's items, alluring in their raw, almost

anti-digital physicality. It's a cottage industry that adds a *samizdat* mystique to a countercultural scene that is more insolent than it is subversive.

One of the figureheads of this alternative scene is Yan Cong, whose go-to protagonist is a chubby, unkempt, middle-aged man. In "Uniqlo Superman," he plods naked into a clothing store and leaves the changing room wearing Tweetie Pie boxers, then flies off into the gray sky with a discount poster for a cape. The deadbeats in the majority of these comics are the opposites of the dutiful youngsters that used to throng propaganda posters.

Alternative comics have also been an important outlet for mental health issues that have, until recently, received little attention. Depression and anxiety are estimated to affect up to 173 million people in China, the majority of whom receive no treatment. During the 2020 lockdown a huge number of young people opened up online and offered support to each other as listeners, or "hollow trees," feelings that comic artists have been putting into pictures for some time. *Dawei,* by YiLi, one of China's few female comic artists, follows the exploits of a man with a pigeon head trying to lead a normal life. "Smile!" commands an impatient photographer. "I *am* smiling," says the bird.

Given their popularity among teens, many underground comics are divertingly puerile. The most recent anthology of Special Comix, entitled *Biantai,* meaning "pervert" or "transform," is a collection of oversized posters featuring, among benign entries, bloodied severed limbs, men in gimp suits and heels, girls locked in various sexual positions, and naked people being poked by giant cacti.

Sex has always been a thorny topic. Mainland Chinese media does not have a ratings system, which means that everything

74 effectively has to be child-friendly, but that's not to say there aren't plenty of transgressions. During the Cultural Revolution, romance and sexual relations had been punishable "bourgeois" crimes. Writers such as Wang Anyi took risks in the post-Mao years, intimating repressed and illicit romances in her early fiction. But by 1994, Wang Xiaobo was goading the censors in his novel *The Golden Age*. He highlighted the perverse double standards of officials during the Cultural Revolution who, under the pretense of reforming perpetrators, used people's forced confessions of illicit sexual relationships to arouse themselves. Wang was also one of the first high-profile authors to write about homosexual relationships, in his story "Sentiments Like Water," which was turned into the film *East Palace, West Palace*. "Because they had not spoken out," Wang wrote in a later essay, "other people thought they didn't exist." Then in 1998, a novel called *Beijing Comrades** appeared online and circulated within the Chinese LGBTQ+ community. The book portrayed the romance between a young male prostitute and his first client, a successful businessman. Published under the pseudonym Bei Tong, some speculated that it was actually written by Wang Xiaobo. Others, including the Hong Kong director Stanley Kwan, who adapted the book into a film, refer to Bei Tong as "she," believing the writer to be a sympathetic female friend. The author's identity remains a mystery.

Today, homoerotic romance is one of the most popular and potentially dangerous genres of online fiction in China. And it is predominantly written by "shes." Known in English as "boy's

---

* "Comrade," or *tongzhi,* has become the most commonly used term to identify members of China's LGBTQ community.

love" (BL), in Chinese it has a more beguiling name, *danmei*,
meaning "addicted to beauty" or "aestheticism." Whichever
term you use, it's an intriguing and counterintuitive genre that
consists of male-male romances written by girls for other girls,
and it is much more popular than heteronormative romances.
As long as relationships simmer and never boil over, these
homoerotic narratives are allowed to survive in print and even
thrive in the mainstream. Print versions of the "pure love"
danmei online novel *Run Freely*, by Wu Zhe, have scaled China's
official bestseller charts in recent years.

Imported to the mainland from Japan via Taiwan, where it is
known as *tanbi*, *danmei* fiction is not unique to China, but it has
evolved to both reflect and challenge specific aspects of Chinese culture. There is a general division between *danmei* novels
that are "clearwater fiction" (*qingshui wen*), which are sex-free,
and "flesh fiction" (*rou wen*), which are not—although there
is a vast gray area due to young writers' increasingly elaborate
and playful euphemisms for sex itself. Sex-free boy's love has
thrived in mainstream entertainment, with many *danmei* web
novels such as *Grandmaster of Demonic Cultivation* and *Guardian*
becoming a lucrative feeder lane for popular TV adaptations, in
which the homoerotic element (not to mention anything supernatural or unscientific) is easily removed or re-spun as "socialist
brotherly love." It is a trope that was inadvertently pioneered in
the Mao era, when hyperrealist propaganda posters often featured men holding hands or embracing in their glorious bond
under communism.

Guardian was written by someone who calls herself
Priest, and chronicles the romance between two male superhuman sleuths who investigate supernatural phenomena. Its

76 straightened-up version on TV received more than 52 million views in the first week of its release, its popularity fueled by "Guardian girls" who discussed the homoerotic hints dropped between the male duo. Knowledge of its original erotic subtext was a huge part of the appeal.

On-screen, however, progress is short-lived. In 2016, a high school *danmei* novel adapted for a web series called "Addicted" was canceled after an episode showed two men kissing for the first time. Even though homosexuality was decriminalized in 1997, and declassified as a mental illness in 2001, censors continue to label it a perversion, banning the "presentation or representation of abnormal sexual relationships or acts, including incest, homosexuality, sexual perversion, sexual predation, sexual abuse, and sexual violence." In their latest crackdown, the Chinese government asked television and streaming platforms to ban the appearance of "sissy" and "effeminate" men.

Some have argued that, like communism, this kind of homophobia is actually a Western import. Before the Communist Revolution, it was common in the eighteenth and nineteenth centuries for male patrons to woo young boys playing the *dan*, or female role, in traditional Beijing opera. And from the lyrical Tang dynasty poetry of Bai Juyi, to the sworn brotherhood between the three heroic warlords in the classic Chinese novel *Romance of the Three Kingdoms,* loyalty and platonic love between men had been a time-honored literary trope. One might wonder why, these days, it is heterosexual girls who like to read and write stories about male lovers. Female authors actively write themselves out of their own narratives; the genre's popularity is almost predicated on the absence of a leading female protagonist. As such, *danmei* gives young female writers an ironic freedom. By imagining themselves as men, they escape through fiction the constraints that apply only to girls—namely, hypocritical judgments about sexual transgression, losing one's virginity, slut-shaming, becoming pregnant, the pressure to marry, and choosing between family and a career.

Educated, only-child girls, raised with the same parental pressures and expectations as boys, are tired of the way in which women are portrayed either as "Mary-Sues" (coined in fanfiction to describe overly idealized women without any faults) or as strong, unromantic zealots, the "de-feminized female characters of Maoist Socialist Realism." For a genre that lacks female protagonists, *danmei* novels have become a space for girls that actively excludes male writers and readers. "The *danmei* circle believes that it requires a complete detachment from reality and the male view of sex and homosexuality," said one sidelined male *danmei* author who wished to remain anonymous.

While it is often viewed as LGBTQ+ fiction, *danmei* often strays into cliché when describing "gay" relationships, with an overreliance on "top" and "bottom" characters and, in the case of sexual content, a sadomasochistic dynamic. But the opportunity to see male characters suffer romantically is part of the appeal for some young female *danmei* writers, who self-identify as "rotten girls," or *funu*. Ordinarily in fiction, and in reality, it is the girl rather than the submissive male (*shou*) who is suffering at the hands of the dominant male (*gong*, which in Chinese is a convenient play on "lord" or *zhugong**). The gender of lovers is

* It is hard to ignore that some of China's most prestigious authors, including Jia Pingwa, Ge Fei, Su Tong, Yan Lianke, and Mo Yan, write in varying degrees of sympathy and matter-of-factness about the casual violence, kidnapping, and rape meted out upon women and girls throughout the 20th century.

78   often secondary to the desire to break taboos. "I don't believe in homosexuality," said one young writer arrested for printing obscene content. She said she was "just curious."

Perhaps a transgressive and masochistic view of the world is, for some young female writers, the consequence of feeling frustrated by the conservative and patriarchal expectations placed upon them. The more explicit novels—not easy to find these days—redolent of the Japanese "erogu" (erotic grotesque) and even the "lustmord" of the Weimar era, are intentionally risky, containing dubious consent, rape, male pregnancy, disabled submissive characters, sadism, incest, or sex between stepsiblings.

Some "rotten girls" have paid a heavy price for their transgressions. While several male-authored cultivation novels have been canceled in recent years for violence and/or problematic sex scenes, the punishments for female *danmei* authors have been noticeably more severe. In 2018, Lady Tianyi was sentenced to ten years in jail for her online novel *Occupy*, which describes male—male relations between a teacher and his student. Another woman, Mr. Deep Sea, was imprisoned for four years when she was found selling and signing self-published copies of her explicit novel *The Caged Emperor*.

Many *danmei* writers, for understandable reasons, self-publish their work in zines known as *gerenzhi* (if it's their original creation) and *tongrenzhi* (if it is fan fiction based on TV shows, celebrities, or other novels). The two authors mentioned above, victims of their own success, had "illegally" published and sold more than 5,000 copies of their novels. Controversial topics are generally overlooked by the government as long as they don't sell. But draconian punishment for the most

successful transgressors is a commonplace tactic, reflecting the
Chinese saying: "Kill the chicken to scare the monkey."

In a country that has, in certain regions, started to unofficially
criminalize cultural and religious differences, the idea of being
an honorable outlaw is a very real and dangerous experience for
some of China's ethnic minorities. Not because they have committed any crimes, but because their very ethnicity is deemed
by the state as transgressive. In a 90 percent Han majority
country, some of China's fifty-five ethnic minority groups have
found themselves charged with separatism or terrorism, especially those speaking on behalf of Tibetan or Uyghur culture.

That, or they have been assimilated, the reverse edge of the
blunt sword of Chinese cultural integration, in which traditional ethnic traits are stereotyped and repackaged as proof of
a harmonious relationship with the Chinese state. For example,
in 2012, China Central Television (CCTV) awarded Lhasa, the
capital city of the Tibet Autonomous Region, the strange status
of "happiest city in China." As Jigme Yeshe Lama argues, "happiness" dominates media depictions of Tibet, in which the CCP's
economic investments—roads, urban planning, social welfare,
education, "safety and harmony"—are provided as the reason
life in Lhasa is so "happy." For many ethnic Tibetans, economic
gains are scant compensation for having their ethnic identity
taken away.

Two stories by well-known Tibetan writers explore the
unwitting or enforced complicity of Tibetans in their own cultural erasure. Poet and dissident activist Tsering Woeser, one of
the few to write in Mandarin, uses her story "Nyima Tsering's

Tears" to deconstruct the trope of the "happy Tibetan." A guile-less and trusting young Tibetan monk, who spends his time showing tourists around a temple, is asked to accompany gov-ernment officials to a human rights convention in Norway, where he is to present a speech written for him that offers proof to the world "that Tibetans had human rights and that their human rights were protected." He is confronted with the stunned and hurt expressions of all the exiled Tibetans in the audience, and comes to realize that he is nothing but a naïve stage prop.

In the magical realist fairy tale "Gang" (meaning snow in Tibetan), by writer and director Pema Tseden, innocence is shown to invite exploitation and eventual destruction. Two children, half-human, half-dream, born of the mountains and with translucent, snowlike skin are symbols of prelapsarian Tibetan culture. They raise money for their impoverished nomadic region by allowing outsiders to photograph them, only for snap-happy tourists to destroy the grasslands they were trying to protect.

On the flip side, stories written by Han Chinese writers have played a controversial role in both the elevation and ero-sion of ethnic difference. Li Juan's sentimental short story "The Road to Weeping Spring" could itself be read as an unintentional fable of cultural colonization, in which a secret oasis in the Gobi Desert—frequented by Kazakh nomads for centuries and used as a hiding place for Kazakh leader Osman Batyr—is eventually discovered by a Chinese couple, who decide to stay put and build a restaurant there. Li Juan lived among Kazakh nomads in Xin-jiang's remote Altay region, and her work undoubtedly reflects a deep appreciation for their culture. And yet, as she herself admits, "as a Han Chinese, I describe this unfamiliar landscape,

and no matter how close I am, I am still an outsider." Li originally   81
described Osman as the "bandit chief," enraging Kazakhs who
regard Osman as a hero for opposing the Communists in 1951.
Although she subsequently changed his nickname to "King
of Altay," it's a reminder that the stories we inherit naturally,
and unconsciously, shape the way a fluid collective memory
coalesces into culture.

Bruce Humes, one of the most devoted translators of ethnic
Chinese fiction, links Li Juan's veneration within China's literary circles (she has won several mainstream awards) with government policy, highlighting how easily even well-intentioned
authors inevitably authorize, rather than simply describe, the
correct version of Chinese history and culture. Some have
even made a lot of money from it. Fiction about, rather than
by, ethnic minorities has been some of the most successful
in mainland China's publishing history. Jiang Rong's controversial 2004 novel *Wolf Totem* is often said to be second only
in circulation to Mao's once compulsory *Little Red Book*. The
semi-autobiographical novel follows a city boy "sent-down"
during the Cultural Revolution to live with the nomadic communities of Inner Mongolia. He becomes enamored of the
fierce, freedom-loving "wolf spirit" of the Mongolians, and con-
temptuous of the agrarian "herdlike" Han Chinese. *Wolf Totem*
was intended as a thinly veiled polemic against Han hegemony:
"It doesn't matter if it's farmland or pastureland, forest or river,
city or countryside; all they want to do is mix them all up to
create a 'unified flavor.'"

Jiang Rong, who blamed events such as the Cultural Revolution on China's lack of democracy and what he described as the
"sheepish" nature of the Chinese people, was later revealed to

82   be a prominent Tiananmen Square dissident named Lu Jiamin, who is ethnically Han. His representation of Mongolian culture is seen by some as both intellectually iffy and politically damaging, especially when the young Han protagonist in the novel becomes the torch-bearer of Mongolian culture, at their request:

> There are so many things you Chinese don't understand. You read books, but what you find in them is false reasoning. Chinese write their books to advocate Chinese causes. The Mongols suffer because they can't write books. If you could turn into a Mongol and write books for us, that would be wonderful.

Wolf Totem's legacy, including its blockbuster movie adaptation, has inadvertently been seen as a call to arms for Han dominance. "Wolf culture" is now ubiquitous, with a slew of lupine-themed self-help books and business manuals piggybacking on the success of *Wolf Totem*, not to mention the recent nationalist action movie franchise *Wolf Warrior*. The phrase "wolf warrior diplomacy" is bandied around to describe Beijing's more combative world presence; tech giant Huawei's success has been credited to its "wolf culture," which has, in turn, been described as "the desire to conquer, the worship of power and, in China, [the belief] that 'money is everything.'" Jiang's reductive "wolf" and "sheep" metaphors have contributed to what many see as a predatory and merciless presence in ethnic borderlands.

Inner Mongolian author Guo Xuebo deeply resents the false attribution of "wolf culture" to Mongolian people. He describes

wolves as "greedy, selfish, cold, and cruel," and says that "advo-
cating the spirit of wolves is [a kind of] fascist thought that
goes against humanity." It also goes against ethnic diversity, and
reaffirms the need "to safeguard the history of our ancestors and
our ethnic culture." According to Wang Lixiong, an ethnic Han
democracy activist and author of the 1991 science fiction novel
China Tidal Wave, the surge of Han culture in China's semiau-
tonomous regions has already overwhelmed ethnic minority
history and culture. He believes that Han Chinese immigration
is the government's preferred method of control in "separatist"
ethnic regions. "Inner Mongolia is considered the most successful," he says, "It has a population of about 25 million and 20
million are now Han . . . so the government feels that basically
there is no minority problem in Inner Mongolia."

The situation could not be more precarious for China's 12
million ethnic Uyghurs in the northwestern autonomous region
of Xinjiang, which in Mandarin means "new frontier." Their
language is Turkic in origin, and very different from Chinese.
The majority are Muslim, and a tiny group have committed
deadly terrorist attacks. And yet the very act of writing in their
native tongue can lead to their "disappearance" into one of Xinjiang's well-documented detention or, as the CCP calls them,
"re-education" camps. The long list of imprisoned publishers,
scholars, poets, and writers includes, Ablet Abdurishit Berqi
(pen name Tarim), Adil Tuniyaz, and Aburehim Heyit, while
Haji Mirzahid Kerimi and Nurmuhemmet Tohti have died in
prison. This is far from a roundup of dangerous terrorists and
criminals, but what has been widely referred to as "cultural
genocide," with an estimated 1.8 million detainees.

The consequences of speaking plainly, let alone in one's mother tongue, are increasingly an existential threat. Tarim, who is currently detained, usually writes about love in Uyghur, yet in Chinese his words are focused and political:

> Friends say
> the beauty of Chinese
> is its subtlety
> I ask
> Is that because there is no freedom of speech?
>
> Friends say
> Chinese poetry needs metaphor
> I ask
> Is that the same as a bat liking the dark?
>
> Friends say
> You are too blunt
> I ask
> is daring to speak the truth
> not poetry?

On a little street in Istanbul, there is an independent bookshop and publishing house called Taklamakan, which has become a Uyghur literature "seed vault," devoted to preserving physical copies of Uyghur poetry and prose, now that the works are no longer available in China, and many of the authors no longer free.

With echoes of Woeser's story of scripted happiness, the Xinjiang authorities have invited journalists to witness the benign beneficence of the CCP in these "re-education" camps. Quickly dubbed "Potemkin-façades," they are filled with young, happy "students" who have "volunteered" to learn the Chinese language, Chinese law, and Xi Jinping thought. It's all painted smiles and visible strings. No coincidence, perhaps, that the architect of Tibet's beefed-up police state, Chen Quanguo, was made party secretary of Xinjiang in 2016, and the following year the camps vastly expanded.

The concept of "reform through labor" and "re-education" is by no means new in China. Under Mao, it gave rise to a brief but revelatory genre of fiction in which former detainees of the anti-rightist camps, such as Cong Weixi and Zhang Xianliang, made their names writing "high wall literature" that exposed the humiliations and impotence of the gulag system. "Re-education" camps, both then and now, are not places of rehabilitation, but of subjection.

The Code of Law
Crime, Corruption, and Surveillance

"Twenty years have passed, and life has been rendered one
hundred percent safe, cleansed of all risks, dangers, and perils.
It seems we're left with nothing."
—Han Song, "Security Check"

Law enforcers in China like to keep a clean slate. So much so
that there are, apparently, no unsolved murders, not since 2002,
when police simply stopped logging them. "So they said they
solved every murder case, which is actually an impossible thing
in criminology," according to Børge Bakken, former director of
criminology at Hong Kong University.

Even if the official crime statistics haven't been falsified in
the manner or scale suggested, the draconian efficiency of law
enforcement within China still poses its own unique challenges
to the crime writer. The certainty of the official record and the
draconian efficiency of law enforcement undoubtedly makes
life tough for a crime writer. Writing a murder mystery in a
country that either denies their existence, or through stringent

surveillance makes them nearly impossible, could be a political act by definition. For novelists, this can be bewildering. "When you write crime novels you know you shouldn't write anything too negative," says crime writer Zhou Haohui. "But you have no way of knowing where the line is."

In Zhou's bestselling 2014 novel *Death Notice*, an arch criminal called Eumenides—named after the Greek furies who thirst for revenge in *The Oresteia*—is motivated by the police department's inability to solve crimes. The villain humiliates the elite police unit, teasing them with "death notices" detailing the who, what, where, when, and how of the next murder, and targets people, including a beloved cop, who he believes are responsible for all the police unit's unsolved crimes and murders. Eumenides not only manages to evade capture each time, but cracks cases that the special task force, trained at the best police academy, have failed to close. The bewildered police suspect a criminal this good must have once been a cop himself. This blurred line between cops and robbers, goodies and baddies, underpins the entire novel. The culprit will, of course, be brought to justice at the end of the trilogy—that's the golden rule of crime capers. But the high-wire act performed by Zhou Haohui in *Death Notice* was his ability to spin out the chase without overstating police ineptitude or entirely focusing on the turgid procedural dance of the investigating officer or judge, as is the case in much of China's traditional crime fiction narratives.

China has one of the oldest legal traditions in the world, shaped by the twin forces of Legalism (social control through law and punishment) and Confucianism (social control through moral teaching). These coexisted in the detective stories of Detective Dee and Judge Bao, some dating back to the thirteenth-century Yuan dynasty. Their popularity marches on to this day in lengthy TV, manga, and comic book adaptations. Known as "magistrate's desk" fiction, these harsh but fair judges are cele-brated for bringing down crooked politicians, helping peasants overcome injustice, exposing false confessions, and settling domestic feuds, one of which provided the inspiration for Ber-tolt Brecht's *The Caucasian Chalk Circle*.

However, with the fall of the Qing dynasty and a symbolic end to feudalism and autocracy, these long-standing legal and narrative traditions became tangled in the wheels of China's twentieth-century constitutional mayhem. Under Mao, a codi-fied rule of law was replaced with a subjective rule by law, which culminated in anti-rightist purges, the dismantling of the judi-ciary, and the violent mob justice of the Red Guard during the Cultural Revolution. It also meant that crime fiction vanished: Given that crime was clearly the product of unjust bourgeois and capitalist societies, it was irrelevant in Mao's law-abiding socialist society.

Fast-forward to the present day, and crime novels negotiate the twin forces of commercialism and propagandism, or the public's desire for entertainment and the state's desire to sani-tize it. In fact, the term "crime fiction" is not widely used at all. Following the Tiananmen protests in 1989, in which students called for economic reform, democracy, and the rule of law, a lot of Chinese crime fiction or "legal system literature" turned into a new type of "public security literature." It became a genre that was less about criminality than about law enforcement. Law and order are the pillars of the current administration. And their enforcers—judges, police, lawyers, security agents—have been told to "resolutely put absolute loyalty, absolute purity, and absolute dependability into action," according to the minister of public security Zhao Kezhi. In other words, legality is loyalty.

This is not necessarily a new development, but the swift passage of Hong Kong's National Security Law in July 2020, in which social institutions and individuals now face criminal charges for any acts deemed to "endanger" national security, demonstrates both a clear-eyed commitment to enforcement of the law, and a lack of clarity about what is unlawful. As Amnesty International points out, the charge of "subversion" as something that endangers national security "can mean virtually anything." Much like writers navigating censorship's moveable and invisible goalposts, the law can feel at once discretionary and absolute.

Unsurprisingly in this climate, domestic writers of crime or public security are likely to depict law enforcers in a positive light. Fiction is expected to reflect "reality," but it can also act as a proxy for actual justice. This demands a correlation between fiction and reality that sinologist Jeffrey Kinkley defines as "law as literature," as opposed to "law in literature."

The most successful example of "law as literature" was a 2017 TV show called *In the Name of the People,* based on author Zhou Meisen's internet novel of the same name about an anti-corruption police unit. It was a cultural sensation at the time. Both the book and screenplay seamlessly mirrored Xi Jinping's anti-corruption campaign, a sweeping crackdown on "tigers and flies" (swatting both powerful and low-ranking officials) that has seen more than 1.5 million officials "sanctioned" since it was kickstarted in 2012, including the high-profile takedown of the former Communist Party Secretary of Chongqing, Bo Xilai.

90   One of the reasons for the TV show's success was that there had been an unspoken embargo on any coverage of high-level corruption stories on TV since 2004. This was the first time in years that audiences had seen corruption acknowledged as part of "main melody" programming. Zhou Meisen, who also scripted the TV show, praised the Supreme People's Protectorate for actively encouraging him to write about corruption at a national level, and even claimed to be surprised when the censors did not change anything in his script, given the sensitive nature of official corruption as a subject. The show, in the view of both Zhou and the state-backed *Global Times*, could "lead to a golden age for anti-graft productions."

Zhou's glorification of the flawless and indefatigable anti-graft unit can also be seen as the epitome of state power. *In the Name of the People* might be more accurately rebranded *In the Name of the Police*. "Public security literature," says Kinkley, could be "the ultimate police-state fantasy—writing China's crime fiction themselves." In other words, the state only decided to acknowledge the existence of corruption by kicking its ass.

The show's popularity also reflected a much-needed catharsis for audiences, who got to see smug, dirty politicians get pinned like worms. The first takedown in *In the Name of the People* is inspired by a well-known news story in which an official was found to be hiding so much cash that investigators burned through four counting machines when toting it up.

These days, both the CCP and its critics view the obscene wealth of public officials as an aberration. How writers in either camp explain it, however, is what sets them apart. Main melody narratives such as *In the Name of the People* tend to depict the corrupt as rotten apples that have fallen a long way from an

upright, healthy tree. The novelist Ning Ken, however, suggests
that high-level corruption is less an anomaly than it is a systemic blight. Publicly shaming a handful of officials is a cursory
attempt to explain away the everyday graft that pervades public
life: He draws a direct line between high-level abuses of power
and pervasive grassroots issues, which include air pollution and
food safety scandals. It's one of the reasons he thinks that China
needs a new type of literature, one he dubs "ultra-unreal," or
chaohuan fiction.

In the fiction of Murong Xuecun, corruption is not so much
commonplace but inescapable. In his novel *Dancing Through
Red Dust*, a lawyer, once nicknamed "the Pillar of the State" for
his lofty idealism, quickly becomes a crooked, callous wom-
anizer who tampers with evidence, hides his assets, and pays
people off with Louis Vuitton bags. The second half of the novel
takes place in a fearsome remand center in which the incarcer-
ated lawyer finally comes to understand the corrupt system for
which he has become a sacrificial lamb, and which continues to
line the pockets of those in higher places. "In the world of TV,
the good are rewarded for their virtue and the bad are caught in
the net of the law," he realizes. "In my world, villains are never
punished—they rule the road."

Some survivors of the anti-corruption campaign have
become audacious and wanton fiction writers. Wang Xiaofang
personally experienced a workplace governed by graft, connections, and kickbacks. He left his job as a civil servant—or, as
he referred to himself at that time, a "spiritual eunuch"—after
his boss, the deputy mayor of Shenyang, was executed for gam-
bling away $3.6 million of public money. Wang's novel, *The Civil
Servant's Notebook,* is a funny and unsettling glimpse into the

92   farcical world of provincial mayoral elections. "In politics," says
the narrator, "the best way of protecting yourself is to yell 'stop
thief!' while picking your neighbor's pocket." Everyone, from
incumbent mayor to lowly pencil pusher, deploys dirty tactics
and suffers humiliating setbacks in their race to the bottom. A
bureaucrat even drinks his boss's urine every day in the hope
of getting a promotion. Wang insists, simply, that his absurdist
novel "told the truth." And, given that he was not implicated
in his boss's criminal dealings, the book received an unexpected endorsement from then-premier Wen Jiabao. The censors simply waved it through as a cautionary tale of how not to
behave.

One figure, both writer and lawyer, stands out as a true
idealist. He Jiahong is a teacher of law at the prestigious
Renmin University in Beijing, and has written extensively
about wrongful convictions and forced confessions in life and
in fiction. Most of his novels follow Hong Jun, a "gentleman
lawyer" or *junzi,* who devotes himself to helping ordinary citizens obtain justice, usually for crimes they didn't commit. This
peculiar legal paradox is often reflected in his titles: *Innocent
but Corrupt Officials, Innocent Murder.* His clients always *seem*
guilty. In *Hanging Devils,* based on a true story, a young man has
already confessed to the murder of a young woman, and in *Black
Holes,* an avaricious young trader is falsely accused of corporate
fraud. The gentleman lawyer calmly sniffs out the truth.

He Jiahong's optimism makes him somewhat of an out-
lier in the crime-writing world. His novels are neither propa-
gandistic nor critical. Instead, he believes passionately in the
efficacy of China's legal constitution, adopted in 1982, if only
it were properly enforced. He claims to offer recommendations

for how to deal with miscarriages of justice, while reminding everyone that "it's a challenge for all human societies." Still, any suggestion that the government needs to be reminded of its own constitution is potentially risky. Article 35, for example, states that "Citizens of the People's Republic of China shall enjoy freedom of speech, the press, assembly, association, procession, and demonstration." All of these things are routinely censored, including the word "constitution" itself.

Anti-capitalist counter-espionage novels, the only genre that even Mao didn't ban, remain a safe port for contemporary crime writers. Inspired by their Soviet predecessors, these novels were initially used to glorify the Party. Today, China's most successful spy novelist, Mai Jia, largely focuses on counter-espionage during the Republican era of 1912—49. His books are so popular that, for a time, he was projected to do for Sino-spy fiction what Henning Mankell did for Scandi noir. Unlike Le Carré—style cat-and-mouse intelligence operations, Mai Jia's books are ponderous, often rather surreal, depictions of a life lived as an invisible and impersonal instrument of the state.

His communist-era story *Two Young Women from Fuyang* reads almost like a pastiche of a murder mystery. A People's Liberation Army officer investigates what could be dubbed "the case of the broken hymen." Following a medical exam, a female army recruit has been dismissed on two charges: she is not a virgin (poor moral conduct) and she claims she has never had a boyfriend (lying to the army is the same as being unfaithful to the Party and the people). She insists upon her purity, but ends up committing suicide. The PLA soldier eventually proves the dead woman's innocence by finding a human error in the

94   records: hymens are like fingerprints, says the doctor who carried out the initial examination, and the broken one wasn't hers.
The discovery results in a sentence of death by firing squad for
the woman with the real broken "virtue". While it is hard to tell
if this was Mai Jia's intention, this bizarre story—recounted
in factual, almost naïve reportage—has the feel of a satire, a
send-up of a system in which justice and punishment is more
important than either the truth or the fairness of the laws that
system upholds.

One of the most illuminating novels to emerge in the last
ten years is former policeman A Yi's *A Perfect Crime* (the Chinese
title was a quote from Anthony Burgess's *A Clockwork Orange*:
"What's it going to be then, eh?"). It is more of a *whydunit*, an
examination of the role of retributive justice. Drawing upon
Dostoevsky's *Crime and Punishment* and Jim Thompson's *The
Killer Inside Me*, the novel follows a bored young man who cal-
lously kills a sweet-natured classmate, and then goes on the run
before giving himself up and confessing. With the interrogators
unable to understand his motive, it is only when they offer him a
reduced sentence on the condition that he change his story that
the killer exhibits his first true sense of despair: He wants to be
punished for the correct crime.

Unlike Dostoevsky, there is no attempt at a moral solution.
Although the killer is sentenced to death by firing squad, it is
only on account of his perverse integrity; he would rather stand
by his crime in all its intentional senselessness than submit to
a corrupt plea bargain. The fact that *A Perfect Crime* passed by
the censors is both proof that censorship guidelines are not as
predictable or pervasive as we might expect, and that a morally
ambiguous message is permissible as long as the case itself is

closed and justice is seen to be done. A Yi was asked to make one
tweak to the story, relocating the action to an unspecified city,
without having to alter the underlying disaffection of the character or the desperation of the worldview.

Crime in China, perfect or otherwise, is indeed very scarce rela-
tive to most international metrics. Still, according to Amnesty,
each year the state is estimated to execute more people than the
rest of the world combined.

    The sense of security created by low crime rates explains, in
part, why intrusive policing and ever-expanding state surveillance seems to be broadly welcomed rather than feared by most
Chinese people. In fact, the international uproar over China's
social credit system (a national scoreboard of people's social
reputation) was largely ignored by those actually affected by it.
According to a wide, independent study by Dr. Xinyuan Wang
at UCL, most Chinese people support it, believing it will keep
them safe from things like fraud and petty crime. While this is,
in part, thanks to the tightly controlled and relentlessly patriotic state media, for some, the desire for safety at the expense
of privacy, apparently, can be traced back to memories of law-
lessness during the Cultural Revolution. Scarred by the frenzied
denunciations between friends and family, interviewees in the
study said they welcomed omniscient, objective surveillance as
a way to counteract malicious gossip. "People are doing things,"
so the saying goes, "and the sky is watching."

    The nature of policing in northwestern China, referred to
as the Hanopticon (a play on Jeremy Bentham's Panopticon),
is widely seen as dystopian science fiction put into practice.
Orwellian thought-police track what people read and who they

96   talk to; reeducation camps prevent rather than punish insur-
rection among ethnic Uyghur and Kazakh minorities, chan-
neling the idea of "pre-crimes" in Philip K. Dick's "The Minority
Report."

Increasingly, science fiction is the only genre that can keep
up with the startling reach of policing and surveillance. Chen
Qiufan, one of China's most exciting, and prolific, young science fiction writers, is fascinated by the psychological impli-
cations of this constant, intrusive mental analysis. In his short
story "Balin," a mythological creature's excessive empathy—
manifest in its ability to mirror a person's actions without time
delay—poses unsettling questions about the nature of human
agency. "If we can't distinguish between mechanical imitation
and conscious, willed movement at the level of neural activity,
then the question is: Does free will truly exist?" In another of
Chen's stories, "A Man Out of Fashion," the answer is firmly no.
The future is governed by a ruling elite in space that uses technology to control their citizens' every move; rebellion, revolution, and love are all carefully planned illusions.

Given the intimate nature of the latest surveillance technology, in which all human behavior can be logged, stored,
and scanned, it is not inconceivable that, in the near future,
every crime may in fact be solved or preempted after all. The
alleged fiction of China's perfect homicide statistics may soon
become fact. But even then, while technology will be able to
tell us exactly where, when, and to whom crimes are scheduled
to take place, we may still look to art and literature to learn and
wonder why.

Back to the Future

Longing for the Past, Gazing at the Stars

"The desire to revive the old ways seems to be matched in
strength by the desire to reject reality . . . a popular wave of
nostalgia is often the precursor to social change."
—Xu Zhiyuan, *Paper Tiger: Inside the Real China*

Here's a modern fairy tale. A teenage orphan, mistreated by her
stepmother, leaves home in rural western China to begin a new
life in the city. She moonlights as an electrician, a waitress, and
a DJ. Having just started to make strides in her music career,
she hears that her beloved grandmother is ill, and abandons her
dreams and returns to the small village, where she finds fame
and fortune as the world's most successful "rural influencer."
This tale of reverse migration belongs to Li Ziqi, who has been
making mesmerizing films about her "rural life" and uploading
them to Weibo, Douyin, and YouTube since 2015. She tills the
fields, shucks corn, and hacks and hauls bamboo to make furni-
ture. She harvests silk from silkworms for quilts, tints her lips

98   with rose petals, and prepares traditional homegrown delicacies in a basic kitchen—all without a hair out of place.

Li is the world's most successful pioneer of a modern paradox: using social media to extoll the virtues of a life without modern technology. "Postmodernism is what you have when the modernization process is complete and nature is gone for good," Fredric Jameson said. And the majority of Li's 50 million viewers are under no illusion that her rural idyll is real life. In fact, it evokes one of China's most enduring literary fables, "The Peach Blossom Spring," written in 421 by the poet Tao Yuanming, about a hidden agrarian utopia. "There's no use telling outsiders," warn the people who live there; the catch with any utopia or "no place," is that you can't find it in reality. Li Ziqi offers a way for urban youngsters to imagine how things should be by imagining how they once were, an idealized past and future forged in an imaginary present.

The "cottagecore" craze—known in China as *fugu* ("nostalgia for traditional ways")—exploded all over the world during the 2020 lockdowns. As people sat in pokey apartments mainlining bucolic bliss on their smartphones, the urban dream lost its sheen. It might not seem to be what the Chinese government had in mind, having put all its weight behind urbanization and flipping the country in a matter of decades from a rural agrarian society to a metropolitan market economy, one in which 60 percent of the people now live in towns and cities. But Li Ziqi's global appeal has been hailed as a dream come true for state propaganda. "Without a word commending China," declared CCTV, "Li promotes Chinese culture in a good way and tells a good China story."

The concept of the pastoral remains an incredibly powerful force in the Chinese imagination, as both political and literary fiction. The countryside is, of course, the locus of the Chinese Communist creed. Maoism was built upon the revolutionary potential of China's largely agrarian society. Unlike Russia's post-industrial proletarian revolution, Chinese propaganda posters foregrounded farmers driving a tractor with one hand and waving the Little Red Book in the other. Today, Xi Jinping's own rural biography is integral to the Party's national mythos, and devotional flocks of tourists make pilgrimages to the cave in which he lived for seven years. It was during his time as a "rusticated" youth in remote Shaanxi province that President Xi not only found his communist faith, but also his love of reading, when he famously made a nine-mile trip to borrow a copy of Goethe's *Faust*. The countryside is a key staging post in the great leader's origin story.

President Xi's time in rural Shaanxi differs from much of the fiction and nonfiction written by fellow "rusticated" youths, for whom the destruction of the countryside—both as a result of Mao's radical agricultural policies and the rapid industrialization of the last forty years—has become a pertinent allegory for the loss, rather than the discovery, of their communist ideals. However, unlike the European Romantics and American Transcendentalists who questioned the pervasive idea of man's dominion over nature only when industrialization was in full swing, communion with the natural world—known as "harmony between heaven and humans"—has always been (with the exception of the Maoist era) the very essence of art in China. It was, and still is, the inspiration for China's ink-and-wash paintings, calligraphy, and poetry. Even China's ideographic writing system has an organic relationship with the natural world. "East 東," for example, is an image of the sun in the trees to convey sunrise.

Widespread urbanization, even in rural areas, has also led to a physical and mental state of philosophical dislocation that writer Xu Zhiyuan describes as a "lost frame of mind." He says that the "meaning behind old trees, flowing water, *jueju** poems, moonlight, and temples has all vanished, to be replaced by tall buildings, neon lights, automobiles, glass, metal, cement, profits and earnings, and high interest rates. I do not know how to extract poetic meaning from those things." He captures the widespread feeling of exile felt by people in China who long for the ancestral villages that they've never visited. It's a sense of spiritual displacement that, ironically, reconnects writers and poets to their ancient literary heritage. Yearning for one's native home is a beloved cliché in Chinese poetry, immortalized more than a thousand years ago by the Tang masters Li Bai and Du Fu. Two of their most famous poems, "Quiet Night Thought" and "Moonlit Night," which are still memorized by schoolchildren, use the moon as a symbol of homesickness in exile.

Broken Wings, the 2016 novel by China's "peasant literati figurehead" Jia Pingwa offered (perhaps unwelcome) validation for all those migrants who have left the countryside—and a reality check for those urbanites who've never lived there. Since all the young women have fled to the city, Jia depicts "wifeless villages" as spiderwebs from which young men struggle to escape. Single men left behind are known as "bare branches," and they consume

---

* A four-line poem popular in the Tang dynasty (618−907).

"blood onions" (named for their deep crimson flesh) to boost their virility, only to suffer sexual frustration and long-term despair when they fail to find a partner. Latent violence and misogyny thrum just below the surface, breaking through when a migrant girl is kidnapped and sold to one of the men. She is locked up, married off, raped, and forced to bear a child. Jia never condones this kind of violent behavior or mindset, but urbanization is seen as the root cause of these problems, and the parasitic city feeds on every aspect of country life, albeit from afar. The "bare branches" that Jia refers to are not just men without a family, but rural villages without growth. "Today, the land that former generations of writers, and I myself, have written about, as well as the familiar countryside that gave us spiritual succour, has been transformed beyond recognition," Jia said. "No matter how hard we look for it, it is gone for good; all our efforts to recapture it will just sound like delirious ravings."

This warning has not stopped people from trying to build utopian communities in China's countryside, via books. The Bishan Project in rural Anhui, launched by a group of intellectuals, called for people to permanently join a community of artists away from cities. Built around ideas of anarchism, communal living, and rural reconstruction, they renovated Bishan village's ancient buildings, turning one into an exquisite bookshop and library, believing that if they build it, people would come.

And for a time, they did. So much so that it became a problem. Chinese authorities quickly shut down events and meetings at the rural commune. One of the intellectuals who started the Bishan Project, Ou Ning, an artist and founder of the literary magazine *Chutzpah!*, documented their constant struggles in his book subtitled *How to Start Your Own Utopia*. The moral of the story seems to be, sadly, that you can't. At least, not now. Ou Ning, who remains disarmingly optimistic, also finds himself in urban exile from his rural Bishan home these days, and the village has instead become more of a gentrified weekend getaway for tourists.

Architecturally beautiful bookshops and libraries continue to pop up all over China in remote villages, as if books somehow herald the effort to resurrect a bygone idyll. An old clifftop house has been transformed into a bookshop in a tiny mountain village perched above the clouds in Chenjiapu, Zhejiang Province, surrounded by free-range chickens, open gullies, paddy fields, and croaking toads. All of its books, thousands upon thousands of them, were transported across vast distances before being carted by hand up the final hill. At the entrance, entire bookcases are dominated by Party-authorized titles—including *Seven Years as an Educated Youth,* a series of interviews with locals in rural Shaanxi Province about President Xi's time there. The floor-to-ceiling wooden bookshelves frequently double as backdrops for dutiful boyfriends conducting their girlfriends' social media photoshoots. It is hard not to feel that bookshops have become a mix of mausoleum and mirage in the inescapable digital age.

In cities, the future for bookshops hangs in the balance. They are everywhere, but only a few feel like the real deal. One Way Street in Beijing is an inspiring, homegrown cultural hub. It has its own dynamic quarterly literary magazine called *Dandu,* or "independent reader." Nanjing's Librairie Avant Garde, a converted underground carpark and bomb shelter, draws thousands of visitors through its cavernous entranceway via a huge, illuminated cross—books as a spiritual guide in the dark. Shenzhen, the city of migrants, has the largest bookshop in the world, but also the tiny and crammed Old Heaven Books staffed by eager young bookworms.

But elsewhere books are largely symbolic. In some urban spaces, they are not real at all. Inside Tianjin's stunning Binhai Library, meticulously terraced books ripple from floor to ceiling into the shape of an eye. It is literature as art installation—the spines of the "books" are fake, mostly printed on aluminum plates. Similarly in Hangzhou's XL-MUSE bookstore, a wall of mirrors gives the impression of never-ending bookshelves, an accidental homage to the Christopher Nolan science fiction blockbuster *Interstellar*, in which the infinite, floating library is a wormhole between the past and the future.

In the last fifteen years, Chinese science fiction has gone into overdrive. But the genre is hardly a new phenomenon, having become popular at the end of the Qing dynasty and the early Republican era, with Lao She's 1932 *Cat Country* considered one of the earliest examples. A dystopian critique of the Nationalist government about a society of Martian Cat People hooked on opium-inspired "reverie leaves" and foreign ideas such as "Everybody Shareskyism," Lao's novel was seen as an allegory for Chinese civilization in decline, and one that became an even more accurate prediction of the brutality meted out during the early years of communism. Lao She's prescience did not serve him well, however. Having been purged during the Cultural Revolution, he committed suicide.

Back then science fiction was pioneered as a way to help people "wake up from their 5,000-year-old dream of being an ancient civilization," says Xia Jia, a young writer celebrated for

104   her "porridge sci-fi," a term she coined to capture the melding
       of science, folklore, and fantasy. And Bao Shu (who started out
       writing Liu Cixin fan fiction), has warned against a future that
       repeats the damage of China's recent revolutionary past. His
       story "What Has Passed Shall in Kinder Light Appear," named
       after a Pushkin poem, marches backward through the last sixty
       years of Chinese history as if it is heading into the future, and,
       faced with the prospect of the Cultural Revolution returning,
       warns against the false allure of nostalgia if it prevents society
       from moving forward. Both Bao Shu and his protagonist are on
       thin ice: The narrator befriends dissident Lu Xiaobo, exposes
       the caprice of the Communist Party, and openly names spe-
       cific politicians and policies. It's one of the few science fiction
       stories that has been banned, along with another of his called
       "Songs of Ancient Earth."

           Science fiction usually flies above the political turbulence
       that agitates other genres of fiction. But writers like Han Song,
       considered one of the "three generals" of Chinese science fic-
       tion, often uses science fiction to critique technological prog-
       ress itself. "Science, technology, and modernization are not
       inherent in Chinese culture," he says. "They are like alien enti-
       ties. If we buy into them, we turn ourselves into monsters."

           This anxious link between industrialization and science
       fiction can be traced back to Mary Shelley's *Frankenstein*. Like
       Shelley, Han Song takes pity on the monsters that rampant new
       technologies have thoughtlessly created, seeking out their ves-
       tigial humanity, and even beauty. In "Submarines," the children
       of migrant workers, who live on polluted, twinkling canals sur-
       rounding the city, have evolved amphibious bodies, much to
       the fascination of wealthier urban children. In one of his most

famous stories, "Regenerated Bricks," rubble containing the
human remains of the thousands of people killed in the 2008
Sichuan earthquake is recycled into "intelligent" bricks that are
used for space colonization, leaving the universe haunted by the
ghosts of the earthquake's victims. People are required to shift
or shed their physical form, becoming ghosts in the machine.
Human physiology is another outdated piece of hardware in
need of an upgrade.

Transhumanism, or the symbiotic pairing of a mind with a
computer, which renders the body obsolete, is a recurring theme
in Chinese science fiction, and is often used as a metaphor for
the way in which an inhuman system constructs and shapes
people's narratives. In Nian Yu's story, "In Search of Your Memories," a middle-ranking civil servant lives as a disembodied
transhuman whose happiness is overseen by a jobbing admin-
istrator. Without his own physical muscle memory, he is left
haunted by the feeling that something is missing, which turns
out to be true. A careless edit has irretrievably removed memories of his twin, who died when they were young, leaving him
confused and inexplicably bereft. It's up to readers to decide
whether this is a criticism of systemic amnesia among Chinese
civil servants, or a broader observation that individuals are routinely at the mercy of impersonal, unaccountable algorithms.

Many writers are genuinely concerned about humani-
ty's relentlessly self-centered instincts. In Hao Jinfang's "The
Loneliest Ward," people lie in bed being drip-fed positive feedback until they die, while in Xin Xinyu's "Farewell, Adam," they
surrender their youth to become part of an amalgamated personality for a teen idol. In the ironically titled "The Path to
Freedom," by Tang Fei, a family that quarantines in the hope of

surviving environmental apocalypse outside discovers, too late, that by avoiding biohazardous air, they have failed to evolve the gills and yellow pus required to survive it.

There is sometimes an almost providential form of evolutionary class justice in which the most vulnerable and exploited members of society become its survivors, if not its saviors. In Chen Qiufan's eco-science fiction novel *The Waste Tide*, migrants live on a garbage island, sorting through electronic scrap piles filled with the world's discarded prosthetics, phones, and sex toys. All the while the workers are exposed to horrendous levels of pollution, and their blood becomes more and more contaminated with heavy metals. When one girl is infected with a virus that manipulates the metal in her blood, however, she is suddenly able to commune with, and then mobilize, the collective consciousness of her oppressed fellow waste workers, albeit with tragic consequences for her own well-being. Forging a damning link between global markets and the outsourcing of environmental degradation, the novel suggests, maybe even demands, that there should be a future reckoning for the inequity of the present. And this connection between internal human desolation and environmental decay recurs in Chen's work. In a story called "The Smog Society," he even proposes that it is in fact our own unhappiness, a product of consumerism and greed, that is polluting Earth's atmosphere.

If the future only contains people who are either destroyed or destructive, it is perhaps no surprise that caring would be outsourced to automata. This is rarely presented as something to fear, however, and many science fiction writers seem genuinely excited and unusually optimistic about the potential gains of a post-humanist future. Far kinder than their human creators, robots provide tender, filial care to the elderly in "Tongtong's Summer," written by Xia Jia, and therapy for the depressed and suicidal in "Mrs. Griffin Prepares to Commit Suicide Tonight," written by A Que. In Chen Hongyu's "Western Heaven," a science fictional reworking of the Chinese literary classic, *Journey to the West*, a troupe of robots set out to find their human creators, who, hundreds of years after plundering and then abandoning Earth, are now in a faraway universe but just as mercenary and self-serving as ever. The robots arrive back on Earth to find it once again a verdant paradise. The story's hero is a robot created by an aging (human) artist who, wishing to immortalize human art before the Exodus, stored thousands of songs, poems, artworks, and pieces of music in the robot's memory. The sad plight for this abandoned, artistic little machine is that, surrounded by robots that were built for entirely practical uses, he alone struggles to understand his purpose.

The role and value of art is always put to the test by technological advances and political imperatives. But just as governmental strictures often lead to experimental new forms in literature, so many Chinese science fiction writers seem commendably intrigued by the opportunities and challenges that the intersection of technology and literature may bring. Xia Jia imagines a dispiriting future in which the artistic criteria for good poetry are reprogrammed in order to prove that machines are more poetic than humans in her story "The Psychology Game." And yet, such is the dizzying pace of change in contemporary China that this has already happened in real life.

In 2018 a literature competition was set up using an "AI judge" to compare thousands of stories that had appeared in China's literary journals. Originally the AI program had been created to hunt for new TV and film adaptation ideas by "reading" China's millions of online novels, many of which are themselves millions of words long. The bot had pretty good taste: A short story by Mo Yan placed second and Chen Qiufan's "The State of Trance" took first prize. The catch is that Chen had written his story, in part, with the use of a deep-learning program. In other words, the algorithm "liked" algorithmic fiction the most, which included sentences like this:

> But this begins with the turn of the real mathematical power, it is very hard to lose the afterward, to change the future's website, as well as assisting the surface of ceremony, pretending that it is somewhere concealed, but can only face crowds.
>
> An authentic tumor.

The gibberish was spoken to a man who just wanted to return a library book. "You stop trying to understand," says the narrator. "Profoundly meaningful, brilliantly insightful, totally incomprehensible dialogues."

It is testament to the tenacity of fiction as a medium that Chen, who studied literature at the prestigious Peking University before working in integrating marketing communications at Google and Baidu, and so many Chinese scientists, astrophysicists, engineers, and coders, are moonlighting as writers. After graduating from university, Liu Cixin, China's bestselling, Hugo award–winning science fiction author, worked as a computer engineer at a power plant in Shanxi into his late forties, long after his novels had become blockbusters. His day job served as a foundation for fiction that is rooted in "hard" science like particle physics, quantum mechanics, and computational mathematics. Liu Cixin's in-depth scientific knowledge makes his noticeably infectious optimism about the future and the role of individual agency within in it all the more beguiling. In his story "Moonlight," Liu simply imagines a man phoning himself from the future with the technology to prevent the destruction of our planet from fossil fuels.

Despite the epic ideas that power most of his stories, there is often an intimacy, even a romance, to Liu's work; an infectious, Carl Sagan—like sense of wonder pervades his writing and characters. In "Sun of China," a migrant worker, who drives tiny tractors that polish the surface of a vast artificial sun, built to change the climate of our parched planet, falls in love with his quiet view of the universe. Once Earth is restored, he elects to sail the retired "sun" into space, knowing he'll never come back. In Liu's hands, this decision is far from bleak. Passing up the chance to return home is a small price to pay for the chance to explore the stars. "I have a horrible dystopia in my mind," Liu once said. "In that future of our inward-looking civilization, the ecology of the earth will be restored. You will have reforestation and the best ecological surface of the world. But across this world, you will not be able to see any single human individual. Instead, there will only be a huge cave, in which you have a supercomputer. Within that supercomputer, there are 10 billion human beings. And these 10 billion human beings are happy. For me this happiness is horrible."

The "horrible happiness" offered by synthetic experiences also extends to synthetic art—it can be technically perfect but, without a human source, it is soulless. In "The Poetry Cloud," a scrawny thirty-year-old man is forced to somehow

110 prove the value of human poetry in order to avoid being tossed into an incinerator. It's a showdown between David and Goliath, art and science. The lowly human is a teacher of classical Chinese poetry on a feedlot that breeds humans for dinosaur consumption; these futuristic "dinosaurs," having discovered that a peaceful mind makes human meat taste better, use poetry teachers to tranquilize the minds of human cattle and, therefore, tenderize their flesh. The human's judge is an omnipotent, arrogant God who floats around as an immaterial geometric shape because it likes "to be concise." But when the teacher shows the God a poem by China's own master of concision, Li Bai, the God is so impressed by its deceptive simplicity that he clones Li Bai to write "every possible poem." This will prove technology is mightier than art. The problem is that the God— and his Li Bai clone, having created an almost infinite number of linguistic combinations, can't figure out which poems are any good. The clone can't write Li Bai's poems because art is expressed through a singular perspective making finite choices, rather than a universal processor making infinite computations. It is proof that, as readers, and as food for dinosaurs, humans raised on literature do indeed have better taste. They may even have a more meaningful future.

Conclusion

"I can't find anywhere else to put my crazy ideas."
 —Wang Xiaobo, *The Silent Majority*

In Hao Jingfang's Calvino-inspired story "Invisible Planets," a space traveler regales their listener with tales of all of the fascinating planets they've visited. There's the planet of liars, in which the only thing that matters is telling an interesting story; the planet where everyone is a visitor; and another where people don't stop growing, leaving the old too tall to communicate with the young. Each time a planet reveals its imperfections, the listener interrupts the storyteller and asks for a different one, not wanting to hear anything too gloomy. While each of these fictional worlds could be interpreted as metaphors for an aspect of Chinese society—propaganda, migration, the generational divide—the entire story seems to be a reflection upon the act of storytelling itself, on a shared search for, and the impossibility of ever settling upon, one perfect world or one perfect narrative.

The fiction discussed in this book emerged at a time of rel-
ative cultural, economic, and political stability in contemporary
China. The restlessness of the post-Reform years had settled
into a confident stride. The country's extraordinary transformation, reflected in its gleaming skylines, seemed nearly
complete. Chinese mainstream culture had itself become big
business, boosted by a vast new consumer class of urban youngsters. Hollywood producers continued to fall over themselves to
secure coveted co-productions and tie-ins, while Chinese life-
style apps like TikTok and WeChat look set to dethrone global
influencers such as Facebook and Twitter as Gen-Z's medium of
choice. The China Dream, as an economic construct, was coming
true. In broad political terms, this has become a blue-sky narrative to which people can pin their pride and patriotism, curated
through state-run media, main-melody programming, and
ubiquitous but discreet censorship.

For writers, who are by nature intuitively tuned to the
hidden influence of any master narrative, this time of economic
ascension has been both liberating and crushing. Back in 2012,
Yan Lianke wrote about returning to his rural home during Chinese New Year, when his family implored him not to get on the
wrong side of the government. "Our lives are good," said his
brother. "Isn't that enough?" And, having been surrounded by
their warmth and love for a few days, it was time for him to drive
back to Beijing:

> As I drove, tears streamed down my face for no apparent
> reason. I just wanted to cry. Was it for my mother, my
> brother, my relatives and the strangers who forget about
> their dignity as long as they have enough to eat? Or for

people like me who worship rights and dignity but live the
life of a stray dog? I don't know. I just wanted to cry out loud.

Three years later, Yan published—in Taiwan, not on the mainland—his novel *The Day the Sun Died*, in which an author called "Yan Lianke" returns to his childhood village, only to discover its inhabitants caught in the grip of a sleepwalking epidemic. It is no accident that Yan's waking dream coincides with this period of prosperity. Once practical and essential needs are catered for, as capitalist societies know firsthand, the lure of consumerism homogenizes and numbs society, replacing complex and disparate individual stories with the collective desire for financial security and more stuff.

Literature has had a tough time in this pragmatic and aspirational marketplace. It is estimated that fiction only makes up about 7 percent of the printed books sold in China, while a third of the market goes to self-help books. Many of these are translated titles from Japan and America. (Self-help books make up 6 percent of nonfiction printed books in America.) There are a few notable homegrown successes: *Seven Years of an Educated Youth* about President Xi Jinping's early years is officially considered the definitive self-help manual.

Unable to promise any material or social gains for themselves or their readers, writers of fiction have questioned their own art form in recent years. "Growing up in China, I had been taught to be patriotic and responsible. What value does my writing have if it doesn't do my country any good?" wondered author Qian Jianan, after receiving a barrage of online abuse from cyberbullies—sometimes referred to as "flesh-searchers" in the PRC—for a piece she wrote in English for *The New York*

Times while studying literature abroad. The irony was that her article lamented her inability to be of practical use to her ill mother in Shanghai, having, she says, spent too much time when she was younger writing fiction and not enough time cultivating the necessary connections—known as *guanxi*—to secure her mother top medical care. Her desire to be a writer had, in part, unintentionally made her helpless both as a loyal daughter and as a patriot.

And yet perhaps this is the fate of the writer everywhere, to resist the temptation to create art that serves a personal or political function. It is a temptation that writers are always faced with, to bow down to their own internalized, intrusive reader, be that in the shape of a government, one's family, an ideology, or a Twitter mob. "Writers may feel obligated to 'correct' for the prejudices of the past," added Qian. "They believe that their writing should reflect their values or group identity. Feminists may avoid showing any female character that is too frail or emotional; minority writers feel the urge to present a positive picture of their ethnic group. As a result, fidelity takes the form of loyalty; art serves as the handmaid of collective values."

Fiction allows writer and reader to communicate safely and privately beyond the instant and noisy realm of incessant commentary and political interference. "How to converse with others using personal experience is, I believe, the most crucial reason for the existence of the novel under our current heightened systematization," said novelist Li Er. And it would benefit us as foreign readers wanting to understand Chinese society— as well as our own—to seek out fictional worlds, rather than the broad-brush political and economic narratives of the public domain.

Literature is perhaps the art form most able to resist the
kind of oversimplification required by polarized political
debate. While it can be tied up with social, political, and economic ideas, it also stands as what literary critic Cai Xiang says
is an "independent system" that builds "a structure of feeling." It
is this that creates space to fully engage with the cognitive dis-
sonance at the heart of any culture or society.

The West is contending with its own corrupted political
landscape, fueled by the toxic influence of fake news, conspiracy
theories, and attention-devouring technology. We too are having
to confront our own nations' historical injustices, which, if not
officially censored, have been grossly and sometimes willfully
neglected. We too are trying to understand and manage our own
relationship with free speech and a free press in the age of social
media. And the guiding principle of an attention economy that
rewards outrage over understanding is to be purposely exposed
to things we vehemently agree or disagree with.

Of course, conservative culture warriors have been a little
too eager to draw parallels between the persecution of intellectuals by young, zealous Red Guards during the Cultural Revolution, and the supposed cancel culture stoked by dogmatic
liberals. Nevertheless, everyone should read the English translation of Liu Cixin's breathtaking opening chapter to *The Three-
Body Problem*, in which an astrophysicist is persecuted and
murdered by students for his "reactionary" interpretation of
Einstein's theory of relativity. Before he is killed, the astrophysicist's young accusers inform him that the correct philosophy of
Marxism should have guided his scientific experiments. "Then
that's the equivalent to saying that the correct philosophy falls
out of the sky," he replies. "This is against the idea that truth

emerges from experience." Political absolutism demands the repudiation of context or experience, rendering any kind of moral or physical relativity obsolete.

Literature, or at least the best literature, emerges from experience, too. It is worth mentioning that in the Chinese version, this harrowing chapter is tucked away somewhere in the middle of the book as a flashback, a reminder of the ways in which certain experiences or periods of history can—and sometimes must—be hidden or downplayed in Chinese fiction. While *The Three-Body Problem* is a science fiction blockbuster about alien civilizations competing for universal supremacy, Liu traces the origins of these epic events back to the emotional fallout from this singular, human experience during the Cultural Revolution: The astrophysicist's young daughter witnessed her father's senseless persecution, and lost her faith in the future of humanity itself.

It is hard to say what the future holds for Chinese fiction writers at this time of fractious global politics. Encouraged by the emergence of Trump's post-truth America and the seeming fragility and ineptitude of democracy in times of crisis, the CCP's authoritarian tactics have intensified. Citizen journalists have been arrested and jailed for their reports during the Wuhan outbreak. Xinjiang's "re-education camps" have been widely viewed as proof of the CCP's desire to control any dissent through active oppression and domestic spin. The number of artists, writers, publishers, booksellers, and intellectuals detained—already the highest in the world—on charges of "subverting state power" or "picking quarrels" is climbing. The National Radio and Television Administration have banned artists with "incorrect political views" and "wrong moral standards" from working in the industry. And the enforcement of the National Security Law in Hong Kong has clarified to the world what Chinese governance looks like when democratic liberties are removed.

The writing has been on the wall, especially in Hong Kong. Five members of Causeway Bay Books, known for gossipy titles about CCP leaders, disappeared in 2015, only to reappear on the mainland performing scripted and stage-managed confessions. By 2020, any books that might offend the CCP, including those by or about pro-democracy movements, were pulled from many bookshops in a preemptive bid by publishers and booksellers to save themselves from retroactive punishment.

While it is mainly nonfiction writers and publishers that have felt the sting of these crackdowns, it is uncertain what effect the loss of Hong Kong as a safe port—and, by extension, Taiwan, which watches nervously—will have on the PRC's literary landscape. Hong Kong has been a dependable loophole for domestic writers to publish novels that would not see any light on the mainland. If, as a result, authors are forced to use only Western publishers, they will not only be left with their work appearing mainly in translation rather than in their mother tongue, but also risk inevitable accusations of betrayal. And it will be a tragedy if, like Fang Fang, the "battlefield diarist" in Wuhan, Chinese authors are once again forced to sit on an unambiguous axis of dissident or patriot. This false dichotomy diminishes what is most precious about their fiction in the first place: room for subjective, flawed, ordinary experience.

The hope is that this book has managed to show the ways in which growing prosperity and widespread satisfaction— neither untrue, nor the whole truth—have created both intriguing obstacles and opportunities for writers of fiction in China. Against the ballooning, homogenous mainstream, their narratives so often become instinctively alternative; whether it's young writers turning to fantasy or satire to sublimate feelings of unease and failure at this heralded time of uplift; or science fiction writers, living through a time of technological proliferation, imagining futures that are both brighter and more disturbing than the present.

Whether or not Western readers, and the Chinese government itself, will come to appreciate fiction's unique value remains to be seen. But, unlike the now-or-never nature of much nonfiction, literature can wait until readers are ready for it. In Jia Pingwa's story "The Ugly Stone," a misshapen lump of rock, resented by everyone in its vicinity for having no practical value, is ignored outside a family's house for years, slowly accumulating weeds and lichen, until one day a scientist tells them that it is an asteroid. Over time, the family understands, or maybe decides, that it is beautiful and precious. For governments and corporations insisting on a party line, literature is an unsightly and unwelcome boulder, while for people seeking unusual ideas or experiences outside their own orbit, it is a comet that has fallen to Earth. Who knows what trace elements it may contain of other worlds that we have not yet considered?

This short book took a little longer to finish than I expected. I'd like to blame the delays of the first COVID-19 year but it was mostly due to the seemingly limitless number of books and stories I felt I should be reading, not knowing when to stop or what to leave out. I owe everything to all the Chinese writers whose work has made this such a challenging, and rewarding, endeavor. And apologies to so many brilliant authors—such as Qian Jianan, Lu Nei, Xu Zechen, Zhang Yiwei, Yan Ge, Zhou Kai, Ren Xiaowen, Hao Jingfang, and Fang Fang, to name a fraction—to whom I would have liked to devote more space.

Chinese is a demanding and beautiful language, and translating it into English without losing much of its intrinsic quality is very tricky. I'd like to pay special tribute to all the dedicated translators of Chinese fiction, in particular to Eleanor Goodman, Ken Liu, Carlos Rojas, Allan H. Barr, Jeremy "Deathblade" Bai, Howard Goldblatt, Anna Holmwood, Annelise Finegan Wasomen, Jeremy Tiang, Chloe Estep, James Trapp, Shelly Bryant, Dylan Levi King, Orion Martin, Olivia Milburn, Bruce Humes, Jack Hargreaves, Julia Lovell, Eric Abrahamsen, Michelle Deeter, Poppy Toland, Harvey Thomlinson, Helen Wang, Flora Drew, Josh Sternberg, Theodore Huters, and Canaan Morse who made the task of finding and reading much of the fiction included in this book so much easier—I am grateful for your help on this reading journey. Equally, I owe a huge debt to my wonderful Chinese teachers at SOAS, the Hutong School in Beijing, and ICLP in Taipei, who have helped me navigate the highs and lows of learning Mandarin over the years.

I would not have reached this point without having had the chance to work with Erica Wagner and Tom Gatti at *The Times,* who were talented and inspiring mentors, and also gave me my first opportunities to write about Chinese literature and arts. Thank you in particular to journalist and friend, Sophie Elmhirst, who put me in touch with Columbia Global Reports in the first place. I am hugely grateful to my literature professor at SOAS, Xiaoning Lu; artist Ou Ning; writer and translator Nicky Harman; editor of *Dandu* magazine, Wu Qi; and former head of Penguin China and Pixie B founder, Jo Lusby, for their generous guidance and recommendations in the early stages of research. Thank you to Paul Morris, Luo Jian, Qian Yang, Rosie Blau, Alexandra Robson, Sophie Vickers, Becca Ratcliffe, and Janet and Jamie Basden who, unbeknownst to them, have helped me at various points along the way. And thank you especially to everyone at Columbia Global Reports—Jimmy, Camille, Allie, and Nicholas—for your help and support with this book, from start to finish, and to artist Jo Zixuan for her beautiful cover.

A few final mentions . . . to Nicky Sayers, Lucy Davis, and Caroline Jacomb, whose friendship so often lifts my spirits. To my wonderful sister Rachel, thanks for being such a sparky and original ally over the years. Mum and Dad, this book, along with most things that mean anything in my life, is for you. My dearest Bobby, I hope we get to take you to Beijing and Taipei soon. And finally, to Tom, whose thoughts, support, and companionship I could not be without—thank you for everything.

Paper-Republic.org—the first stop for anyone wanting to read many of the latest short stories being written in China.

Paper Tiger: Inside the Real China by Xu Zhiyuan (trans. Nicky Harman and Michelle Deeter)—essays by a brilliant writer, thinker, and observer of contemporary China.

China in Ten Words by Yu Hua (trans. Allan H. Barr)—a young bookworm starved of books during the Cultural Revolution, Yu explores with humor and insight his own relationship with China's evolving social and political climate.

Why Fiction Matters in Contemporary China by David Der-wei Wang—a fascinating examination of the way twentieth-century Chinese intellectual and literary history continues to influence political and artistic discourse.

Paradise-Systems.com—a Brooklyn-based indie publisher of experimental and off-key Chinese comics, all translated into English.

"The Moon Is Beautiful Tonight: On East Asian Narratives" by Qian Jianan—so far, only a few of her stories have been translated, but Qian is a thoughtful and talented novelist whose nonfiction articles in English, as above, are a treat.

Anything by Yan Lianke—he's a genius.

Love in the New Millennium by Can Xue (trans. Annelise Finegan Wasmoen)—not easy to summarize, or read, but Can Xue offers unparalleled rewards for anyone willing to dive in.

Clarkesworld magazine—its website has an excellent and constantly updated selection of new Chinese science fiction.

Iron Moon: An Anthology of Chinese Worker Poetry (trans. Eleanor Goodman)—a remarkable compendium of poetry by migrant workers living at the coal face of China's epic transformation.

A Hero Born by Jin Yong (trans. Anna Holmwood)—this new translation finally offers English speakers a chance to understand why Jin Yong, a writer in the sixties and seventies of thrilling *wuxia* stories, became China's most beloved author.

Encounters with Chinese Writers by Annie Dillard—a short, delightful book about Dillard's experiences as part of a delegation of artists sent to Beijing in 1982.

Morning Sun: Interviews with Chinese Writers of the Lost Generation by Laifong Leung—a candid and moving collection of interviews with writers in the nineties who struggled to make sense of their shattered socialist ideals.

Chinese Literature: A Very Short Introduction by Sabina Knight—for anyone hoping to get to grips with 3,000 years of Chinese literature, in only 120 pages, this nuanced and illuminating book is essential reading.

Peach Blossom Paradise by Ge Fei (trans. Canaan Morse)—the first novel in Ge Fei's award-winning Jiangnan trilogy, in which a young girl's hapless fate becomes symbolic of the hopelessness and hypocrisies of political and utopian ideology at the turn of the twentieth century.

Invisible Planets: 13 Visions of the Future from China (ed., trans. Ken Liu)—an eclectic and engrossing mix of stories by some of China's most exciting science fiction writers.

Half a Lifelong Romance by Eileen Chang (trans. Karen S. Kingsley)—this masterpiece of thwarted love set in 1930s Shanghai is a wonderful introduction to one of the finest writers of the twentieth century.

The Vagrants by Yiyun Li—a brutal, beautiful debut novel set in a small town in the aftermath of the Cultural Revolution, Li writes with astonishing precision and depth in English, her second language.

The Age of Ambition by Evan Osnos—one of the most important books for anyone wanting to understand China in the twenty-first century, brought to life by Osnos's rich storytelling, rigorous research, and seemingly effortless insight.

NOTES

INTRODUCTION

10   **"the sky and ocean are crystal clear today":** Liu Cixin (trans. Chi-Yin Ip and Cheuk Wong), "The Poetry Cloud" in Mingwei Song and Theodore Huters, ed. *The Reincarnated Giant: An Anthology of Twenty-First Century Chinese Science Fiction* (Columbia University Press, 2018), p.143.

10   **"fine art works should be like sunshine from blue sky":** "Chinese President Xi Jinping Warns Against 'Immoral' Art," BBC, October 16, 2014, https://www.bbc.co.uk /news/entertainment-arts -29645574.

10   **"modern art and literature needs to take patriotism as its muse":** "A Year After Xi's Landmark Speech on the Arts, Some Things Get Left Out," *Wall Street Journal*, October 15, 2015, https://blogs .wsj.com/chinarealtime/2015/10 /15/a-year-after-xis-landmark -speech-on-the-arts-some-things -get-left-out/.

11   **the literal and figurative emblem:** David Bandurski, "The Fable of the Master Storyteller," China Media Project, September 29, 2017.

11   **also known as "the weather":** Perry Link, *The Uses of Literature: Life in the Socialist Chinese Literary System* (Princeton University Press, 2000).

11   **or "the gray zone":** Louisa Lim and Jeffrey Wasserstrom, "The Gray Zone," *New York Times*, June 15, 2012.

11   **poet, essayist and novelist Han Dong:** Han Dong (trans. Nicky Harman), "Foggy," *Peregrine: An English Companion to* Chutzpah! *Magazine*, Issue 3, August 2011.

12   **reformist Liang Qichao famously declared:** Liang Qichao (trans. Gek Nai Cheng), "On the Relationship Between Fiction and the Government of the People," 1902. In Kirk A. Denton, ed., *Modern Chinese Literary Thought: Writings on Literature, 1893-1945*, (Stanford University Press, 1996), pp. 74–81.

15   **novels about, say, authoritarian governments:** Amy Hawkins and Jeffrey Wasserstrom, "Why 1984 Isn't Banned in China," *The Atlantic*, January 13, 2019.

16   **established seventy years ago to uphold "literary norms":** Hong Zicheng, "A History of Contemporary Chinese Literature," *Brill's Humanities*, 2007, p. 27.

16   **"looking at the writer, not the writing":** Eric Abrahamsen, "The Real Censors of China," *New York Times*, June 16, 2015.

124

17 **"In writing we have freedom, but in publishing we have discipline":** Yan Lianke (trans. Roddy Flagg), "Darkness Visible," *Index on Censorship*, 2008.

17 **"anaconda in the chandelier":** Perry Link, "China: The Anaconda in the Chandelier," *New York Review of Books*, April 11, 2002.

19 **what Liu Cixin himself calls a kite line to reality:** "To Reach the Pure Realm of the Imaginary: A Conversation with Cixin Liu," *Public Books*, June 1, 2020.

20 **wrote a nurse from Gansu province:** Wei Shuiyin (aka Long Qiaoling) (trans. Josh Rudolph), "Do Not Disturb," *China Digital Times*, February 21, 2020.

20 **in an aphorism for state hypocrisy:** Wang Youwei, "Care from Nowhere," Poemlife.com, February 8, 2020.

21 **he changed tack and wrote a novel instead:** "Yan Lianke and Xiaolu Guo on Writing Through Rural Poverty in China," Lithub, December 27, 2017.

22 **"The pages of George Orwell's *1984* are coming to life there":** "Pompeo Says Orwell's '1984' Coming to Life in China's Xinjiang Region," Reuters, October 11, 2019, https://uk.reuters.com/article/uk-usa-china-muslims-pompeo/pompeo-says-orwells-1984-coming-to-life-in-chinas-xinjiang-region-idUKKBN1WQ29D.

CHAPTER ONE

24 **"Everyone believed in dreams, but didn't believe in reality":** Yan Lianke (trans. Carlos Rojas), *The Day the Sun Died* (Chatto & Windus, 2018), p. 15.

24 **"nipped in the bud, long before it had had time to grow its natural dimensions":** Yu Hua (trans. Allan H. Barr), *The Seventh Day* (Text Publishing, 2015), p. 28.

26 **was not what I intended at all:** "It's Hard to Get My Books Published in China" Interview with Yan Lianke, *The Guardian*, September 22 2018.

28 **"the occurrence of B is completely *unrelated* to A":** Yan Lianke (trans. Carlos Rojas), "Author's Note," *The Explosion Chronicles* (Vintage, 2016), p. 455.

28 **expressed a plaintive hope that readers:** Mo Yan (trans. Howard Goldblatt), "Nobel Lecture," December 7, 2012.

29 **"you mustn't fall into the trap of believing everything he writes":** Mo Yan (trans. Howard Goldblatt), *Life and Death Are Wearing Me Out* (Arcade Publishing, 2008), p. 269.

31 **"I just want to be left alone to work for myself":** Mo Yan, *Life and Death Are Wearing Me Out*, p. 305.

31 "the wild roots growing under the soil of reality": Yan Lianke (trans. Carlos Rojas), *The Explosion Chronicles* (Vintage, 2013), p. 456.

32 "without any concern for getting published": Yan Lianke, "Xiezuo de beipan: 'Sishu de houji'" [A traitor to writing: Afterword to *The Four Books*], in *Dangdai zuojia pinglun* (2013), p. 5.

35 "time will make people forget everything": Ge Fei (trans. Howard Goldblat), "Remembering Mr. Wu You," in Jing Wang, ed., *China's Avant-Garde Fiction* (Duke University Press, 1998).

35 a cricket that lives, sings, and dies in a closed box: Ge Fei "The Invisibility Cloak: An Interview with Ge Fei" (trans. Canaan Morse), *Paris Review*, November 14, 2016.

35 "you might discover that life is actually pretty fucking beautiful": Ge Fei (trans. Canaan Morse), *The Invisibility Cloak* (New York Review of Books, 2016), pp. 125–126.

35 "industriously ploughing through the earth": Annelise Finegan Wasmoen, "Can Xue Interview," Bomb Magazine, www .bombmagazine.org, March 11, 2015.

35 some have dubbed her "inner long march": Annelise Finegan Wasmoen, "Can Xue Interview."

36 "As he spoke the sky was already growing light": Can

Xue (trans. Annelise Finegan Wasmoen), *Love in the New Millennium* (The Margellos World Republic of Letters, Yale University Press, 2018), p. 17.

37 "taut emotional logic": Annelise Finegan Wasmoen, "Can Xue Interview."

37 become estranged because they know each other too well: Can Xue, *Love in the New Millennium*, p. 11.

37 "resembled deserted graves": Yan Lianke, *The Day the Sun Died*, p. 132.

38 "the people who have graves in their hearts": Yan Lianke (trans. Grace Chong), "What Happens After Coronavirus? On Community Memory and Repeating Our Own Mistakes," ThinkChina, March 11, 2020.

38 "a question in our hearts when a lie comes our way": Yan Lianke, "What Happens After Coronavirus?"

38 "You are in a period where the future has come and the past has not yet passed": Porter Anderson, "April 2018 Bestseller Lists from China: Young Readers Cheer a Celebrity-Powered World Book Day," Publishing Perspectives, May 29, 2018, https:// publishingperspectives.com/2018 /05/april-2018-bestseller-lists -from-china-young-readers-cheer

126 -a-celebrity-powered-world-book
-day/.

CHAPTER TWO

39 **"I've been in pain ever since
I was born":** Chen Xiwo (trans.
Nicky Harman), *The Book of Sins*
(*New Writing from Asia*, 2014),
pp. 16–17.

40 **refers to sympathetically
as "groundless rebellion":** Chen
Xiwo, "Discussion: Pain," *Los
Angeles Review of Books China
Channel*, March 1, 2018, https://
chinachannel.org/2018/03/01
/discussion-pain/.

41 **sexuality is his "trademark":**
Porter Anderson, "China's Feng
Tang: Translating the 'Beijing,
Beijing' of His Peers," Thought
Catalog, June 4, 2015.

41 **"the vast world opens the
crotch of its trousers":** "Chinese
Translation of Tagore Pulled for
Sexual Embellishment," *Straits
Times*, December 31, 2015.

41 **known as the "Janus face":**
Ling Yang, "Tiny Times, Persistent
Love: Gender, Class, Relationships
in Post-1980s Bestsellers," in
Wanning Sun, ed., *Love Stories in
China* (Ling Yang), p. 151.

42 **a thrilling and dogged
defender of his apparently
apathetic:** Han Han (ed., trans.
Allan H. Barr), *This Generation:
Dispatches from China's Most*

*Popular Literary Star (and Race Car
Driver)* (Simon and Schuster, 2012).

43 **"This is a failed generation":**
Fu Xiaoling, "Yan Lianke: Post-80s
Are Not So Rebellious," July 27, 2015
(Chinese), https://cul.qq.com/a
/20150727/032896.htm. "The
Post-80s Is a Failed Generation,
Unable to Speak Out," China News,
August 12, 2015.

43 **"somehow maintained
the status of a young person":**
"Zhou Jianing on Contemporary
Chinese Narratives." Transcript
of interview with Chris Merrill at
the International Writers Program,
March 15, 2017, https://iwp.uiowa
.edu/podcast/origins-the
-international-writing-program
-podcast-2.

44 **"How can a poet not spend a
moment considering the fate of
humanity":** Xu Xiao, "Two Poets'
War of Words Shows China's
Yawning Generation Gap," *Sixth
Tone*, February 8, 2018.

44 **"yet still insisting on holding
my head up high":** Xu Xiao, "Two
Poets' War of Words Shows China's
Yawning Generation Gap."

45 **Rather than focusing on
their own desires:** "Intellectuals
Say The Post-80s Generation
Is A Failed Generation," Sina.com.
cn, August 12, 2015, http://finance
.sina.com.cn/china/20150812
/054922940769.shtml.

45   "What should we do to
make him see us?": You Fengwei,
The Loach 泥鳅 (Chunfeng wenyi
chubanshe, trans. Qian Yang),
Urban Strangers in China, p. 211.
December 2014 Dissertation
University of California.

46   tiny gains yielded by his
work underground: Chen Nianxi
"Son" (trans. Eleanor Goodman)
in Qin Xiaoyu, ed., *Iron Moon:
An Anthology of Chinese Migrant
Worker Poetry*. (White Pine Press,
2016), p. 61.

47   "To die is the only way to
testify that we ever lived": Jenny
Chan and Ngai Pun, "Suicide as
Protest for the New Generation
of Chinese Migrant Workers:
Foxconn, Global Capital, and the
State," *Asia Pacific Journal* 8, no. 37,
September 2010, https://apjjf
.org/-Jenny-Chan/3408/article
.html.

47   "I swallowed an iron moon":
Jenny Chan and Ngai Pun, "Suicide
as Protest for the New Generation
of Chinese Migrant Workers,"
p. 198.

48   severs her finger at the end of
a twelve-hour shift: Xie Xiangnan,
"Work Accident Joint Investigative
Report," in Qin Xiaoyu (ed., trans.
Eleanor Goodman), *Iron Moon:
An Anthology of Chinese Migrant
Worker Poetry*, (White Pine Press,
2017), p. 76.

48   "I watched those five youthful   127
years come out of the machine's
asshole": *Iron Moon: An Anthology
of Chinese Migrant Worker Poetry*,
p. 79.

49   "you could be an official if
you wrote good poetry": *Iron
Moon*, documentary, directed by
Feiyue Wu (2016).

51   won Wang Zhanhei the
inaugural Blancpain-Imaginist
Award: "Post-90s Writer Wang
Zhanhei's Debut Work *Air
Cannon* Won the Blancpain-
Imaginist Literary Prize," Xinhua,
September 20, 2018 (Chinese),
http://www.xinhuanet.com/book
/2018-09/20/c_129957751.htm.

CHAPTER THREE

54   "Before any of the legends of
the business world have risen":
Poor Four, *Extraordinary Genius,* on
Qidian.com, https://book.qidian
.com/info/3641743/.

54   "Once my profound
veins are fixed": Mars Gravity
(trans. Alyschu), *Ni Tian Xie
Shen (Against the Gods)*, "Chapter 4:
The Wedding Procession," https://
www.webnovel.com/book/ni-tian
-xie-shen-(against-the-gods)
_20148845705100105/the-wedding
-procession_54086916785632602.

55   "lose themselves in the tide
of market economy": "China's Xi

128   Points Way for Arts," *China Daily*, October 10, 2014.

56   **after Hollywood, Korean idol dramas, and Japanese anime:** Rachel Cheung, "China's Online Publishing Industry—Where Fortune Favours the Few, and Sometimes the Undeserving," *South China Morning Post*, May 6, 2018.

56   **Thrilled by Cazad's rehabilitation from drug addiction:** Charles Liu, "US Man Credits Chinese Web Novels for Curing His Addiction to Drugs," The Beijinger, April 25, 2017, https://www.thebeijinger.com /blog/2017/04/05/us-man-credits -chinese-web-novels-curing-his -addiction-drugs.

57   **"lust of the mind" or "lust of intent":** Heather Inwood, "The Happiness of Unrealizable Dreams," in *Chinese Discourses on Happiness* (HKU Press, 2018), p. 215.

57   **Cao Xueqin's 1792 vernacular novel:** Heather Inwood (trans. David Hawkes, Martin Huang), "The Happiness of Unrealizable Dreams," p. 215.

62   **a vast echo chamber of "prosumers":** Shih-Chen Chao, "Desire and Fantasy On-line: A Sociological and Psychoanalytical Approach to the Presumption of Chinese Internet Fiction," thesis submitted to University of Manchester, 2012, p. 69.

63   **"The novel's ranking, influence, and author's fame":** Yang Chen, "Becoming a Start Level Author," *Book of Authors* (Qidian International).

64   **"I want to influence the world with China's intellectual property":** Li You, "Q&A with Author Zhang Wei on China's Online Literature," Sixth Tone, June 8, 2016.

65   **"cultural proletariat" or "intellectual laborer":** Yu Zhang and Calvin Hui, "Post Socialism and Its Narratives: An Interview with Cai Xiang," MCLC Resource Center Publication, July 3, 2016.

65   **the vast majority of online "writing hands":** Guobin Yang, "The Internet as Cultural Form: Technology and the Human Condition in China," *Knowledge, Technology, and Policy* 22 (2009), pp. 109–115. https://doi.org/10 .1007/s12130-009-9074-z.

65   **"Live your dreams, don't waste your youth":** http://yuewen .com.

65   **"Help readers to fantasize about what they lack":** Yang Chen, "The Three Core Elements of Web Novels." *Book of Authors*.

66   **"How should I punish myself?":** Jack Hu, "The Story Behind China's Online Literature Boom," Global Voices, December 19, 2017.

66   **"This feels worse than being sold into slavery":** Kenrick Davis, "China's Web Fiction Writers Strike Over Copyright Confusion," Sixth Tone, May 12, 2020.

67   **"But they had me fucking cut off the entire fucking trunk":** Patrick Howell O'Neil, "Popular Chinese Online-Fiction Authors See Entire Novels Deleted by Censors," Daily Dot, April 19, 2015.

67   **He calls it "spiritual sublimation":** Xu Ming, "Popular Online Writers Change Genre from Fantasy to Reform and Opening-up," *Global Times*, July 31, 2018.

68   **about a cultural relic restorer:** Wang Ru, "Beijing's Central Axis Runs Through Zhang Wei's Latest Novel," *China Daily*, updated June 24, 2021, http://www.chinadaily.com.cn/a/202106/24/WS60d4434da31024ad0bacb557.html.

68   **"I did not expect to be honorary president":** Zhang Jie and Xun Chao, "Mo Yan, the President of the University of Internet Literature, Said the Boundaries of Writing Are Becoming Increasingly Blurred," West China Metropolis Daily, October 31, 2013, http://culture.ifeng.com/whrd/detail_2013_10/31/30825848_0.shtml.

69   **university's stated aims are:** "Network Literature University,"

Baidu, https://baike.baidu.com/item/网络文学大学/12022265.

CHAPTER FOUR

71   **splitting and splicing individual characters to create new ones to avoid censorship:** Visen Liu, "In China, Internet Censors Are Accidentally Helping Revive an Invented 'Martian' Language," Quartz, July 31, 2017.

72   **"include scenes of violence, pornography, terrorism and crimes":** Karen Ressler, "China Blacklists Attack on Titan, Death Note, 36 More Anime/Manga," Anime News Network, June 9, 2015, https://www.animenewsnetwork.com/news/2015-06-09/china-blacklists-attack-on-titan-death-note-36-more-anime-manga/.89055.

73   **Depression and anxiety are estimated to affect up to 173 million people in China:** "Mental Health in China: Challenges and Progress," *The Lancet* 380, no. 9855 (2012), pp. 1715–1716.

74   **"other people thought they didn't exist":** Wang Xiaobo (trans. Eric Abrahamsen), *The Silent Majority* in *Asia Literary Review*, February, 2008, p. 22 (first published in 1997).

74   **believing the writer to be a sympathetic female friend:** Scott E. Meyers, "Translator's Note,"

130 *Beijing Comrades* (Feminist Press, 2016), p. viii.

76 **banning the "presentation or representation of abnormal sexual relationships or acts":** "General Rules for the Review for the Content of Internet Audiovisual Programs," *Xinhua*, July 1, 2017.

76 **argued that, like communism, this kind of homophobia is actually a Western import:** Thomas Moran, "Homoeroticism in Modern Chinese Literature," in Kirk A. Denton, ed., *The Columbia Companion to Modern Chinese Literature* (Columbia University Press, 2016), p. 337.

77 **women are portrayed either as "Mary-Sues":** Xiqing Zheng in conversation with Henry Jenkins "The Cultural Context of Chinese Fan Culture" (part 3) February 6, 2013, http://henryjenkins.org /blog/2013/02/the-cultural -context-of-chinese-fandom-an -interview-with-xiqing-zhengpart -three.html.

77 **a space for girls that actively excludes male writers and readers:** Yuan Ren, "Where Slash Fiction Makes Dangerous Words," *The Advocate*, November 11, 2014, https://www.advocate.com/print -issue/current-issue/2014/11/11 /where-slash-fiction-makes -dangerous-words.

77 **gender of lovers is often secondary to the desire to break taboos:** Kevin Tang, "Inside China's Insane Witch Hunt For Slash Fiction Writers," Buzzfeed, April 22, 2014, https://www.buzzfeed.com /kevintang/inside-chinas-insane -witch-hunt-for-slash-fiction -writers.

78 **draconian punishment for the most successful transgressors:** Yang Rui and Ren Qiuyu, "Novelist Known for Gay Content Sentenced for 'Illegal Publishing,'" CX Tech, May 21, 2019, https://www .caixinglobal.com/2019-05-21 /novelist-known-for-gay-content -sentenced-for-illegal-publishing -101418063.html.

79 **the reason life in Lhasa is so "happy":** Jigme Yeshe Lama, "Tibet and Happiness in Chinese Media Discourses: Issues and Contestation," in Gerda Wielander and Derek Hird, eds., *Chinese Discourses on Happiness* (Hong Kong University Press, 2018), pp. 44–54.

80 **to deconstruct the trope of the "happy Tibetan":** Jigme Yeshe Lama, "Tibet and Happiness in Chinese Media Discourses," p. 46.

80 **"that Tibetans had human rights":** Tsering Woeser (trans. Jampa, Bhuchung D. Sonam, Tenzin T. Perkins, Jane), "Nyima"Nyima Tsering's Tears," in Tenzin Dickie, ed., *Old Demons New Deities: Twenty-One Short Stories from Tibet* (Or Books, 2017), p. 91.

81   **"no matter how close I am, I am still an outsider":** Ou Ning, "There Is No Best Places and No Worst Place: An Interview with Li Juan," Jiantian Today, September 13, 2012, https://www.jintian.net/today/html/69/n-38669.html.

81   **highlighting how easily even well-intentioned authors inevitably authorize:** Bruce Humes, comments July 7, 2015, *The Road to Weeping Spring* by Li Juan in Paper Republic, June 25, 2015. https://paper-republic.org/pubs/read/the-road-to-the-weeping-spring/.

81   **"It doesn't matter if it's farmland or pastureland":** Jiang Rong (trans. Howard Goldblatt), *Wolf Totem* (Penguin Books Ltd. Kindle Edition), p. 510 of 527. Location 8008 of 8286.

82   **"If you could turn into a Mongol and write books for us":** Jiang Rong, *Wolf Totem*, p. 46 of 527. Location 787 of 8268.

82   **tech giant Huawei's success has been credited to its "wolf culture":** Jianhua Chen (trans. Isabel Galwey), "The Rise of Wolf Culture: Thoughts on *Pleasant Goat* and *Big Bad Wolf*," Association for Chinese Animation Studies, October 16, 2018, https://u.osu.edu/mclc/2018/10/16/the-rise-of-wolf-culture/.

83   **"to safeguard the history of our ancestors":** Laura Zhou, "Wolf Totem: Writer Blasts Hit Film Over 'Fake' Mongolian Culture," *South China Morning Post*, February 24, 2015, https://www.scmp.com/news/china/article/1722433/ethnic-chinese-writer-criticises-fake-culture-forced-mongolians-hit-film.

83   **"Inner Mongolia is considered the most successful":** Ian Johnson, "Beyond the Dalai Lama: An Interview with Woeser and Wang Lixiong," New York Review of Books blog, August 7, 2014.

83   **what has been widely referred to as "cultural genocide":** Catherine Philp, "'Cultural Genocide' for Repressed Minority of Uighurs," *Times*, December 17, 2019, https://www.thetimes.co.uk/article/cultural-genocide-for-repressed-minority-of-uighurs-bpow6dw89.

84   **in Chinese his words are focused and political:** "Tarim Open School of Thought 直白派," in "Tang Danhong: Tarim, a Uyghur," China Digital Times, February 2019, https://chinadigitaltimes.net/chinese/606169.html.

85   **Quickly dubbed "Potemkin-façades":** Magnus Fiskesjö, "Cultural Genocide Is the New Genocide," PEN/OPP, May 5, 2020, https://www.penopp.org/articles/cultural-genocide-new-genocide?language_content_entity=en.

132   85   **"students" who have "volunteered" to learn the Chinese language:** "China Uighurs: Detained for Beards, Veils and Internet Browsing," BBC, February 17, 2020, https://www .bbc.co.uk/news/world-asia-china -51520622.

CHAPTER FIVE

86   **"cleansed of all risks, dangers, and perils":** Han Song (trans. Ken Liu), "Security Check," *Clarkesworld*, August 2015, http:// clarkesworldmagazine.com/han _08_15/.

86   **"So they said they solved every murder case":** Joanna Chiu, "Crime and the Chinese Dream," *Los Angeles Review of Books China Channel*, January 2, 2019, https:// chinachannel.org/2019/01/02 /crime-dream/.

87   **"you know you shouldn't write anything too negative":** Steven Lee Myers, "How to Catch a Killer in China: Another Chinese Crime Novel Goes Global," *The New York Times*, June 4, 2018, https:// www.nytimes.com/2018/06/04 /books/zhou-haohui-death-notice -chinese-crime-thrillers.html.

88   **"legal system literature" turned into a new type of "public security literature":** Jeffrey Kinkley, *Chinese Justice, the Fiction: Law and Literature in Modern China* (Stanford University Press, 2000), p. 301.

88   **"resolutely put absolute loyalty, absolute purity, and absolute dependability into action":** Chris Buckley, "'Drive the Blade In': Xi Shakes Up China's Law-and-Order Forces," *The New York Times*, August 20, 2020 (updated October 14, 2020), https://www.nytimes.com /2020/08/20/world/asia/china -xi-jinping-communist-party .html.

89   **the charge of "subversion" as something that endangers national security:** "Hong Kong's National Security Law: 10 Things You Need to Know" Amnesty International, July 17, 2020, https:// www.amnesty.org/en/latest/news /2020/07/hong-kong-national -security-law-10-things-you -need-to-know/.

89   **"law as literature," as opposed to "law in literature":** Jeffrey Kinkley, *Chinese Justice: The Fiction*, pp. 18–19.

90   **could "lead to a golden age for anti-graft productions":** "Debut of Daring Anti-Graft Show 'In the Name of the People' a Sign That Corruption Genre Is Making a Comeback," *Global Times*, March 27, 2017, https://www.globaltimes.cn /content/1039733.shtml.

90   **could be "the ultimate police-state fantasy":** Jeffrey Kinkley, *Chinese Justice: The Fiction*, p. 20.

91   **one he dubs "ultra-unreal,"
or *chaohuan* fiction:** Ning Ken,
"Modern China Is So Crazy It
Needs a New Literary Genre,"
Literary Hub, June 23, 2016, https://
lithub.com/modern-china-is-so
-crazy-it-needs-a-new-literary
-genre/.

91   **"In my world, villains are
never punished—they rule the
road":** Murong (trans. Harvey
Thomlinson), *Dancing Through
Red Dust* (Make Do Publishing UK,
2015), p. 113.

91   **as he referred to himself at
that time, a "spiritual eunuch":**
"'Civil Servant's Notebook' Author
Sheds Light on Dark Side of Power
in China," Agence-Frenche Presse,
October 14, 2012 (as reprinted in
the *South China Morning Post*),
https://www.scmp.com/lifestyle
/books/article/1060933/civil
-servants-notebook-author-sheds
-light-dark-side-power-china.

92   **"to yell 'stop thief!' while
picking your neighbor's pocket":**
Wang Xiaofang (trans. Eric
Abrahamsen), *The Civil Servant's
Notebook* (Penguin Books, 2015),
p. 78.

92   **The censors simply waved
it through:** "'Civil Servant's
Notebook' Author Sheds Light on
Dark Side of Power in China."

92   **claims to offer
recommendations for how to
deal with miscarriages of justice:**

Owen Bowcott, "We Might Abolish
the Death Penalty in 20 Years: He
Jiahong on Justice in China," *The
Guardian,* October 22, 2016, https://
www.theguardian.com/world/2016
/oct/22/we-might-abolish-the
-death-penalty-in-20-years-he
-jiahong-on-justice-in-china.

93   **are routinely censored,
including the word "constitution"
itself:** Bethany Allen-Ebrahimian,
"On First Annual Constitution
Day, China's Most Censored
Word Was Constitution," *Foreign
Policy,* December 5, 2014, https://
foreignpolicy.com/2014/12/05
/china-constitution-censorship
-rule-of-law/.

95   **to execute more people than
the rest of the world combined:**
"China Named 'World's Top
Executioner' as Global Rate Falls,"
The Guardian, April 12, 2018,
https://www.theguardian.com
/world/2018/apr/12/china-named
-worlds-top-executioner-as-global
-rate-falls#maincontent.

95   **they welcomed omniscient,
objective surveillance as a way
to counteract malicious gossip:**
Xinyuan Wang, "Hundreds
of Chinese Citizens Told Me
What They Thought About
the Controversial Social Credit
System," The Conversation UK,
December 17, 2019, https://
theconversation.com/hundreds
-of-chinese-citizens-told-me
-what-they-thought-about-the

134   -controversial-social-credit
-system-127467.

96   **we can't distinguish between
mechanical imitation:** Chen
Qiufan (trans. Ken Liu), "Balin,"
Clarkesworld, April 2016, https://
clarkesworldmagazine.com
/chen_04_16/.

CHAPTER SIX

97   **"The desire to revive the old
ways seems to be matched":** Xu
Zhiyuan (trans. Michelle Deeter
and Nicky Harman), *Paper Tiger:
Inside the Real China* (Head of Zeus,
2015), p. 118.

97   **as the world's most
successful "rural influencer":**
"Exclusive Interview with Li
Ziqi, China's Most Mysterious
Internet Celebrity," YouTube,
posted September 12, 2019, https://
www.youtube.com/watch?v
=J9CfVcX0Yh4.

98   **"Postmodernism is what
you have when":** Fredric Jameson,
*Postmodernism, or the Cultural Logic
of Late Capitalism* (Duke University
Press, 1991), p. ix.

98   **"Li promotes Chinese culture
in a good way":** Alice Yan, "State
Media Joins Rural Blogger Li Ziqi's
Millions of Followers," *South China
Morning Post*, December 11, 2019,
https://www.scmp.com/news
/china/society/article/3041516

/chinese-state-media-joins-rural
-life-blogger-li-ziqis-millions.

100   **"I do not know how to
extract poetic meaning from
those things":** Xu Zhiyuan,
Paper Tiger.

101   **rural villages without
growth:** Jia Pingwa (trans. Nicky
Harman), *Broken Wings* (ACA
Publishing, 2019), p. 227.

103   **to help people "wake up from
their 5,000-year-old dream":** Xia
Jia (trans. Ken Liu), "What Makes
Chinese Science Fiction Chinese?"
Tor.com, July 22, 2014, https://
www.tor.com/2014/07/22/what
-makes-chinese-science-fiction
-chinese/.

104   **"Science, technology, and
modernization are not inherent in
Chinese culture":** Chitralekha Basu,
"The Future Is Now," *China Daily*,
March 18, 2011, https://europe.
chinadaily.com.cn/epaper/2011-03
/18/content_12192254.htm.

108   **"You stop trying to
understand":** Chen Qiufan (trans.
Josh Sternberg), "State of Trance,"
in *The Book of Shanghai* (Comma
Press, 2020), p. 157.

109   **"I have a horrible dystopia
in my mind":** John Plotz and Pu
Wang, "'To Reach the Pure Realm
of the Imaginary': A Conversation
with Liu Cixin," Public Books,
January 1, 2020, https://www

.publicbooks.org/to-reach-the
-pure-realm-of-the-imaginary-a
-conversation-with-cixin-liu/.

CONCLUSION

112 **implored him not to get on
the wrong side of the government:**
Yan Lianke, "The Year of the Stray
Dog," *New York Times,* April 12,
2020.

113 **is officially considered the
definitive self-help manual:** "Why
Self-help Books Are So Popular in
China," *The Economist*, November
2020.

114 **"Writers may feel obligated
to 'correct' for the prejudices
of the past":** Qian Jianan,
"Mirror, Mirror: On the Nature
of Literature," TheMillions.com,
March 11, 2019.

115 **an "independent system"
that builds "a structure of
feeling":** Yu Zhang and Calvin Hui,
"Postsocialism and Its Narratives:
An Interview with Cai Xiang,"
MCLC Resource Center, June 2018,
https://u.osu.edu/mclc/online
-series/zhang-hui/.

Columbia Global Reports is a publishing imprint from Columbia University that commissions authors to produce works of original thinking and on-site reporting from all over the world, on a wide range of topics. Our books are short—novella-length, and readable in a few hours—but ambitious. They offer new ways of looking at and understanding the major issues of our time. Most readers are curious and busy. Our books are for them.

Subscribe to our newsletter, and learn more about Columbia Global Reports at globalreports.columbia.edu